FODOR'S MODERN GUIDES

are compiled, researched, and edited by an international team
of travel writers, field correspondents, and editors. The series,
which now almost covers the globe, was founded by Eugene
Fodor.

OFFICES
New York & London

Editorial Staff for Bermuda:

Editor: CYNTHIA NELSON

Editorial Assistant: GERARDYNE MADIGAN

Maps and City Plans: CARTER DELAND ASSOCIATES

Drawings: STEPHEN CARTER

Photographs: BERMUDA NEWS BUREAU; STEPHEN CARTER;
TROMSON MONROE ADVERTISING INC.

BERMUDA
1982

ANTOINETTE DeLAND

FODOR'S MODERN GUIDES, INC.
Distributed by
DAVID McKAY COMPANY, INC.
New York

All the following Guides are current (most of them also in
the Hodder and Stoughton British edition).

CURRENT FODOR'S COUNTRY AND AREA TITLES:

AUSTRALIA, NEW ZEALAND
  AND SOUTH PACIFIC
AUSTRIA
BAJA CALIFORNIA
BELGIUM AND
  LUXEMBOURG
BERMUDA
BRAZIL
CANADA
CARIBBEAN AND BAHAMAS
CENTRAL AMERICA
EASTERN EUROPE
EGYPT
EUROPE
FRANCE
GERMANY
GREAT BRITAIN
GREECE
HOLLAND

INDIA & NEPAL
IRELAND
ISRAEL
ITALY
JAPAN AND KOREA
JORDAN AND HOLY LAND
MEXICO
NORTH AFRICA
PEOPLE'S REPUBLIC
  OF CHINA
PORTUGAL
SCANDINAVIA
SOUTH AMERICA
SOUTHEAST ASIA
SOVIET UNION
SPAIN
SWITZERLAND
TURKEY
YUGOSLAVIA

CITY GUIDES:

LONDON
NEW YORK CITY
PARIS

ROME
WASHINGTON, D.C.

FODOR'S BUDGET SERIES:

BUDGET BRITAIN
BUDGET CARIBBEAN
BUDGET EUROPE
BUDGET FRANCE
BUDGET GERMANY

BUDGET ITALY
BUDGET JAPAN
BUDGET MEXICO
BUDGET SPAIN
BUDGET TRAVEL IN AMERICA

USA GUIDES:

USA (in one volume)
ALASKA
CALIFORNIA
COLORADO
FAR WEST
FLORIDA
HAWAII

NEW ENGLAND
PENNSYLVANIA
SOUTH
SOUTHWEST
SUNBELT LEISURE
  GUIDE

SPECIAL INTEREST SERIES:

CIVIL WAR SITES

MANUFACTURED IN THE UNITED STATES OF AMERICA
10 9 8 7 6 5 4 3 2 1

CONTENTS

FACTS AT YOUR FINGERTIPS

FACTS AT YOUR
FINGERTIPS

After you feast your eyes on Fodor...

lend an ear to a Bermudian.

Now that you're considering a holiday in Bermuda, you may have questions even Fodor may not answer.

So if something pops into your mind, call or write us.

Our people, quite understandably, <u>know</u> Bermuda. And we're anxious to help you in any way we can. With a quick and simple answer. With literature about our delightful range of accommodation, including prices. With maps and fact-filled brochures on golf, fishing, sports generally, or honeymoons.

Incidentally, your Travel Agent is also an excellent source of Bermuda information.

We hope you decide on Bermuda. We're very proud of our little island, and we welcome your visit.

Bermuda Department of Tourism

- 630 Fifth Avenue, New York, N.Y. 10111 (212) 397-7700
- Suite 1010, 44 School St., Boston, Mass. 02108 (617) 742-0405
- 300 N. State St., Chicago, Ill. 60610 (312) 329-0777
- 235 Peachtree St. N.E., Atlanta, Ga. 30303 (404) 524-1541
- Suite 510, 1075 Bay St., Toronto, Ontario, Canada M5S 2B1 (416) 923-9600

FACTS AT YOUR FINGERTIPS

PLANNING YOUR TRIP

13.06
5.24
2400
$230

WHAT IT WILL COST. Bermuda is a quality resort with accommodations to fit every pocketbook and life-style. There are simple housekeeping apartments where the manager arranges for your charge account at the local supermarket and lends you a barbecue to guest houses, plain and fancy cottage colonies, and large resort hotels that are almost self-contained villages. Prices in Bermuda are high but you usually get what you pay for—and more. The island has been able to contain her own inflation problem, but can do nothing about the cost of imported food, drink, and furnishings. Therefore, one can expect an annual increase in prices on a par with what has happened in the United States the past 18 months, plus import duties which are high (to replace resident income taxes).

There are excellent packages to Bermuda, especially for golfers, tennis players, honeymooners, and families. Prices tend to drop considerably between mid-November and mid-March and June, September and holiday weekends are busy. Book ahead! Air fares are reasonable from North America and a one-week cruise offers the best of both worlds.

Food, drink, and taxis are expensive but the island's natural beauty is free. You can rent motorbikes by the week and save, or take local buses and ferries which are not only fun, but you get more of a feel for the island. Most of the local beaches are public, and tennis court rentals and greens fees tend to be less than in the U.S. Shopping is a wonderful pastime and British woolens and china are good bargains.

Cost for a Typical Day

A typical day in a luxury resort hotel will cost (one person, double occupancy):

Hotel (includes breakfast, afternoon tea, and dinner)	$85.00
Hotel taxes and service charges	11.50
Tennis court rental, one hour	2.00
Motor bike rental for the day	11.00
Snack at the beach	6.00
Cocktails and entertainment	10.00
Total	$123.50

A typical day in a small, less expensive hotel will cost (one person, double occupancy):

Hotel (includes breakfast, afternoon tea, and dinner)	$60.00
Hotel taxes and service charges	10.50
Tennis court rental, one hour	2.00
Motor bike rental for the day	11.00
Snack at the beach	6.00
Cocktails and entertainment	10.00
Total	$97.50

This can be cut even further by staying in a housekeeping cottage (large) for about $40 per day or a small unit for approximately $30 per day. While food is expensive in the local supermarkets, it is still much less than in a restaurant, and you can take your own snacks to the beach. Guest houses are even more economical, and some offer bed and breakfast for about $35 per day (but no cooking for dinner).

See your travel agent for advice on how to get the most for your money.

WHEN TO GO. Anytime! Bermuda is a year-round resort with a mild, subtropical climate. Winters may be cool and windy but are perfect for golf and tennis and the Department of Tourism has daily events planned for visitors. Spring comes early, and with it the college crowd arrives for five weeks of fun and frolic. June and September are traditional months for honeymooners and second honeymooners return anytime. The official beach season opens the 24th of May and goes through September, but one can swim throughout the year. Most of the hotels and larger cottage colonies have heated pools and some are covered in inclement weather.

The island's summer temperatures are in the 70s and 80s (F.) and the days are generally warm and sunny through November. There has never been a year with less than 340 days of recorded sunshine and the average is 351 days. The lowest temperature officially recorded was 41 degrees F. in 1955 and annual rainfall is approximately 57 inches, spread evenly throughout the 12 months. Rainfall is usually of brief duration and the skies normally clear very quickly. Rain is always welcome on the island as it provides the major source of fresh water.

Monthly Average Daily Temperature

	Air Max. C. F.	Air Min. C. F.	Sea C. F.	Relative Humidity %
Jan.	20.8 (69.4)	15.7 (60.2)	16.7 (62)	77
Feb.	20.0 (68.0)	14.9 (58.9)	16.1 (61)	74
Mar.	20.3 (68.5)	15.3 (59.6)	17.8 (64)	72
Apr.	21.3 (70.4)	15.7 (60.3)	18.3 (65)	74
May	23.5 (74.3)	18.7 (65.6)	22.8 (73)	81
Jun.	26.5 (79.7)	21.4 (70.5)	25.0 (77)	79
Jul.	28.4 (83.1)	23.3 (74.0)	26.7 (80)	77
Aug.	29.4 (85.0)	23.8 (74.9)	28.9 (84)	77
Sep.	28.9 (84.1)	22.7 (72.9)	26.7 (80)	75
Oct.	26.2 (79.2)	21.3 (70.3)	25.0 (77)	75
Nov.	23.3 (73.9)	17.9 (64.3)	21.1 (70)	70
Dec.	21.1 (70.0)	15.9 (60.7)	18.3 (65)	72

Average nightly temperatures are approximately 5°C (10°F) cooler than the daily high temperature.

Month	Sunshine and Rainfall:		
	Daily Average Hours of Sunshine	Monthly Average Rainfall	
		MM	Ins
January	5.1	103.12	4.06
February	5.4	128.27	5.05
March	6.3	117.60	4.63
April	7.5	76.45	3.01
May	8.2	98.04	3.86
June	8.6	131.32	5.17
July	9.9	101.09	3.98
August	9.0	133.86	5.27
September	7.9	133.35	5.25
October	6.3	152.91	6.02
November	5.8	113.79	4.48
December	4.9	97.03	3.82

HOW TO GO. The Bermuda Department of Tourism is one of the most efficient and helpful organizations of its kind in the travel industry. It publishes a number of attractive brochures on Bermuda and stays in close contact with travel agents, keeping them abreast of the latest developments in facilities, rates, and booking trends. Every year, the department invites approximately 1,000 agents from North America, the U.K. and Europe to see Bermuda firsthand. Therefore, the department suggests that you discuss your holiday plans with a travel agent who knows Bermuda and who can contact the department's "Space Service" immediately to find available accommodations. If you do not have a travel agent, the **American Society of Travel Agents,** 711 Fifth Ave., New York, N.Y. 10022; **Association of Canadian Travel Agents,** 130 Albert Street, Suite 1207, Ottawa, Ontario; or the **Association of British Travel Agents,** 53 Newman Street, London W1P 4AH, will advise you.

The following wholesale tour operators have Bermuda package vacations available for sale by retail travel agents. All ground packages include what is specified in the tour brochure and transportation is additional.

U.S. AGENCIES SPECIALIZING IN BERMUDA PACKAGES

Bermuda Playtime Vacations, Inc., 110 East 42nd St., New York, N.Y. 10017 and branches in Boston, Chicago, and Cleveland.
Thomas Cook, 380 Madison Ave., New York, N.Y. 10017 and all

branches. **Haley Corporation,** 711 Third Ave., New York, N.Y. 10017 and branches. **Travel Center Tours,** 5413 N. Lincoln Ave., Chicago, Ill. 60625.

CANADIAN AGENCIES SPECIALIZING IN BERMUDA TOURS

Holiday House, 25 Adelaide St., E., Suite 1301, Toronto, Ont., M5C 1Y2 and in Montreal. **Fairway Tours Ltd.,** 74 Victoria St., Suite 708, Toronto, Ont., M5C 2A5.

U.K. AGENCIES SPECIALIZING IN BERMUDA TOURS

Cadogan Travel Ltd., 159 Sloane St., London, SW1. **Thomas Cook Ltd.,** 45 Berkeley St., London, W1. **Kuoni Travel Ltd.,** Deepdene House, Dorking, Surrey. **R. & O. Air Holidays,** Beaufort House, St. Botolph St., London, EC3A 7DX. **Rankin Kuhn & Co. Ltd.,** 19 Queen St., Mayfair, London, W1X BAL. **Sovereign Holidays Ltd.,** P.O. Box 13, Victoria Terminal, Buckingham Palace Rd., London, SW1. **Speedbird Holidays Ltd.,** 200 Buckingham Palace Rd., London, SW1. **Sunvil Travel,** Sunvil House, 88 Sheen Rd., Richmond, Surrey, TW9.

 HOW TO GET THERE. *By Air: American Airlines* flies daily from New York's Kennedy International Airport, from Newark, Boston, Chicago and Philadelphia. The airline also publishes a beautiful brochure on Bermuda and offers a number of special tours that feature three- to ten-night Holiday Specials, Tennis/Golf or Honeymoon/Anniversary Specials. Round-trip fares available are first class, coach, midweek excursion (Monday through Thursday), and weekend (Friday, Saturday, Sunday).

Delta Airlines flies daily from Atlanta, Boston and Hartford with the same fares available, and has authority to fly from Philadelphia. *Air Florida* flies from Houston and Miami to Bermuda en route to Brussels.

Eastern Airlines flies daily from New York, Philadelphia/Baltimore, Newark/Atlanta, Orlando and Miami. Weekly from Chicago and Detroit. Eastern publishes a brochure called "The Real Bermuda" with three- to ten-night special packages, and includes Bermuda on the airline's unlimited mileage circuit.

Air Canada offers nonstop service from Toronto (4 times weekly in summer; 5 times weekly in winter) with pick-up service in Montreal once a week. The airline also flies nonstop from Montreal 5 times weekly and nonstop from Halifax once a week year-round. Air Canada offers a seven-night Tennis Special Holiday at Elbow

Beach Hotel and three golf vacations at Castle Harbour, Belmont, and Inverurie. Air Canada also flies up weekly from the Caribbean.

From the U.K., *British Airways* flies daily from London, the Caribbean and Central America. British Airways offers special one- and two-week holidays in Bermuda in conjunction with Sovereign Holidays and Seabird Holidays.

The Bermuda government last year relaxed its policy on charter flights and will now permit public charters to call at the island. The charters are permitted from non-gateway cities and from designated gateway cities not served by non-stop scheduled service. The new rules allow many more visitors from North America to enjoy Bermuda.

By Sea: The glamorous days of cruising to Bermuda and back are not over! Between April first and late November, one can board a luxury cruise vessel in New York harbor and sail to Bermuda on a choice of ships while others call at the island from Norfolk, Port Everglades, Miami and European ports. A one-week cruise to Bermuda combines the best of both worlds. On board, there is plenty of time to relax and rest, be pampered by an attentive crew, meet the captain at his complimentary cocktail party, and become acquainted with fellow passengers. One has only to choose the life-style one prefers at sea, whether it be Italian (Home Lines), Dutch/Indonesian (Holland America), or other interesting lines.

Every Saturday during the season, Home Lines' *Oceanic* and new *Atlantic*, and Holland America's *Veendam* and *Volendam* sail from New York about 4 P.M. for Hamilton harbour and St. George's. The vessels arrive in Bermuda early Monday or Tuesday morning for four fun-filled days on the island, and the ship is utilized as a floating hotel (you unpack only once). One can dine on board or try the local restaurants and nightspots. The cruise director's office offers shore excursions daily and shopping on Front Street is just a stone's throw. Golf, tennis, swimming and a variety of water sports as well as motorcycle rentals are all within easy access. On Thursday afternoon, you board your vessel for a leisurely cruise around Bermuda and New York. Back at sea, there is plenty of time to rest up from the active days before arrival in New York early Saturday or Sunday morning.

Home Lines' *Oceanic* also sails every Saturday, offering a day's call in Bermuda en route to the Bahamas. Holland America's *Volendam* sails from New York every Sunday during the season. The Sunday sailings are catching on with honeymooners and Holland America helps spread the joy by presenting the newlyweds with flowers, champagne, a cake, and souvenir cake knife.

Other shiplines that feature calls at the island are Cunard (*The*

Queen Elizabeth 2), Norwegian American Cruises (*Sagafjord*) and P & O (*Canberra*).

The cost of a one-week cruise to Bermuda ranges from $150 to $300 per person, per day (depending upon vessel and accommodations) and includes all meals, plus morning bouillon, afternoon tea, and a sumptuous midnight buffet. It also includes the services of the entire staff and evening entertainment. Extras are tipping, drinks (inexpensive on board), wine with dinner, shore excursions, and port taxes.

 TOURIST INFORMATION. The *Bermuda Department of Tourism* is located in the U.S. at: 630 Fifth Ave., New York, N.Y. 10111; Suite 1010, 44 School Street, Boston, Mass. 02108; 300 N. State St., Marina Towers Bldg. 11th floor, Chicago, Ill. 60610; 235 Peach Tree Street, N.E., Atlanta Ga. 30303. In Canada: 1075 Bay St., Toronto M5S2B1. In U.K.: 9/10 Saville Row, London W1X2BL.

In Bermuda, the department is conveniently located in Old Town Hall, Front Street, Hamilton. *Visitor's Service Bureau* is located at the Ferry Dock in Hamilton, Bermuda Airport, King's Square in St. George's and in the lovely village of Somerset. The *Bermuda Hotel Association* is on Front Street in Hamilton.

The Department of Tourism publishes free of charge "Bermuda," "Bermuda Travel Tips," "Handy Reference Map," "Sportsman's Guide to Bermuda," and many other helpful brochures. In addition, "This Week in Bermuda" and "Bermuda Today" are freely distributed in shops, hotels, and tourist facilities. Cruise passengers will find on board their vessels the free "Bermuda Cruise 1981."

There are excellent bookstores in Bermuda and literature on local history, legend, flora, etc. is abundant. Local historians include William Zuill (director of the Bermuda National Trust) and Terry Tucker, the island's most prolific writer.

 WHAT TO TAKE. The prerequisite for any holiday trip is to pack clothes that are comfortable and easy to wear. In Bermuda, daytime life is informal but dignified and pantsuits for women are de rigueur, but short shorts, bare feet and hair curlers in public are not appreciated. Evening wear is more formal, especially if you are staying in a hotel or cottage colony, and jacket and tie for the men are required in most dining rooms.

The warmer months are from May to November and lightweight

cotton or drip-dry fabrics are most suitable. Men will need a light-weight jacket in the evening and women should bring a shawl or fancy sweater. Bathing suits, tennis and golf clothes, and a light-weight raincoat should also be packed. This is real Bermuda shorts season, especially if you plan to travel around by motorbike (bathing suits, bare feet, or being shirtless are not permitted on cycles).

The season changes from mid-November through April and cloth-ing for cooler weather is needed. During the day, light wool skirts, slacks and sweaters are necessary and the nights are even cooler. But Bermuda weather is variable in any given day and the visitor must be prepared to peel or add layers as necessary. And sudden squalls require a handy, portable umbrella or light raincoat to be carried at all times. Bathing suits, golf and tennis costumes should not be forgotten during the cooler months. Bring a sweater to take off as activity increases.

Should you forget an item, or wish you had another outfit to wear, there are tempting buys in clothes for both men and women. Sweat-ers, skirts, slacks and jackets from Britain as well as resort-type clothes from around the world fill the shops on Front Street and their branches throughout the island. The prices are definitely less than where you came from, and tailoring can be done in a few hours. It is often better to pack too little than too much, and leave room for those tempting buys!

Sports equipment is available for rental throughout the island for golf, tennis, scuba diving and snorkeling, but riding enthusiasts should bring their own gear. Camera buffs need not overload their luggage with film because all kinds of camera equipment can be bought in Bermuda. Many hotels, gift shops, and photo dealers offer one-day service on Kodacolor, Ektachrome and black and white, which can be processed in Bermuda. As the sun is very bright, check suggested settings with a photo dealer or use a light meter.

 TRAVEL DOCUMENTS. Passports and visas are not required except for Iron-Curtain nation-als and Cubans (Cubans holding U.S. residential cards do not require visas). At the time of entry into Bermuda, a return or outward bound ticket as well as proof of citizenship of the U.S. or Canada is required. This proof may be a valid passport, birth certificate, U.S. Naturalization Certificate, U.S. Alien Registration card, or voter's registration card. Smallpox vaccination certificates are required only from travelers who have been in a country which is infected. All bona fide visitors to the colony may remain for a period of three weeks from arrival date.

After this period, they must apply for an extended stay to the Chief Immigration Officer. *Note:* Visitors are not allowed to conduct any business in Bermuda without a special permit and this law is strictly enforced. Contact the Chamber of Commerce (Ferry Dock, Hamilton) for information.

CUSTOMS REGULATIONS. Visitors may bring into the colony, duty-free, all personal clothing, cameras, sports equipment, etc. They may also bring 50 cigars, 200 cigarettes, 1 pound of tobacco, 1 quart of liquor and 1 quart of wine. Importing illegal drugs (marijuana) is an offense and subject to fines of up to $5,000 or 3 years imprisonment, or both. Conviction on indictment carries a maximum penalty of a fine or 20 years imprisonment, or both.

PETS. Permits must be obtained well in advance from the Director, Department of Agriculture, P.O. Box 834, Hamilton 5, Bermuda, for the importation of all animals (including household pets) into Bermuda. Airlines are allowed to carry the pets, either as excess baggage or cargo, but cruise ships are *not*. Dogs and other pets are permitted at some hotels and guest houses but permission must be obtained in advance and only small, well-trained pets are allowed.

MONEY. The Bermuda dollar (BD$) has been linked to the U.S. dollar since August 1977 and is accepted at par in shops, restaurants and hotels. Canadian currency is also accepted but may be discounted. U.K. and all other currencies must be exchanged at Bermuda banks for local tender. U.S. travelers' checks are accepted everywhere. Credit cards may now be used to pay most hotel bills and are accepted in many shops and restaurants.

On the reverse side of all Bermuda notes is a portrait of Queen Elizabeth II. The blue $1 note pictures Bermuda-fitted dinghies racing. The maroon $5 note features St. David's Lighthouse; the mauve $10 note shows the longtail bird. The green $20 note has Somerset Bridge and the brown $50 note features Gibbs Hill Lighthouse. The same picture of the queen that is found on British coinage is also on the reverse side of all Bermuda coins. The 50-cent piece has Bermuda's coat of arms; the 25-cent piece, the longtail bird; the 10-cent piece, Bermuda lilies; the 5-cent piece, the angelfish; and the bronze penny, the wild hog.

TRAVEL FOR THE HANDICAPPED. Senior citizens and handicapped persons are requested to notify the hotel, guest house or cottage colony when requesting space to enable the facility to allocate a suitable room and make any special arrangements that might be required. The large hotels are best suited to handicapped persons since they have large elevators, wider doorways, more accessible bathrooms, and conveniently located public rooms. They provide wheel chairs and have sufficient hotel staff to assist the handicapped.

 RESTAURANTS. One can dine casual or chic in Bermuda, and there is a goodly choice of restaurants in between. A few of the specialty restaurants and hotel dining rooms are excellent, with food, atmosphere, and service on a par with good eating in any major capital. Other restaurants can be disappointing and not worth the high cost of food and drink on the island. But there are Bermudian specialties that should not be missed, like fish chowder, local fish, mussels and lobster, syllabub (a drink of cream and cider), and "Hoppin' John" (black-eyed peas and red rice), as well as Rum Swizzles, which are often the excuse for a party.

If you plan to dine out, advance dinner reservations are suggested and be sure to check on dress requirements. Many restaurants, especially in hotels, require gentlemen to wear a jacket and tie and women to be appropriately dressed in the evening. Dinner menus for the specialty restaurants can run to $60 per person (depending upon drinks and wine); at the medium-priced restaurants from $20 to $25 per person; and at the more moderate restaurants about $15 per person. When the gratuity is not included in the bill, an overall 10 to 15 percent is the accepted amount. (See *Wining and Dining* section for a complete list of restaurants.)

 SIGHTS TO SEE. To complement the beauty of the landscape and beaches, there are many interesting sights to see on the island. There are historic forts *(St. Catherine; Fort Hamilton)* and churches *(St. Peter's; the Cathedral)*, a good climb up *Gibbs Hill Lighthouse* for a bird's-eye view, Botanical Gardens, dolphin acts, 17th-century houses, small museums and galleries, nature reserves, parks and even a perfume factory. There is certainly much to see and do in Bermuda and it's so easy to do it. (See *What to See and Do* section).

CLOSING TIMES. Businesses and shops are closed on the following legal holidays in 1982: New Year's Day; Good Friday, (April 9); Bermuda Day (May 24); Queen's Birthday (second weekend in June); Cup Match and Somers Day (July 29 and 30); Remembrance Day (November 11); Christmas Day and Boxing Day (December 25 and 26).

Businesses and shops are open from 9:30 A.M. to 5:30 P.M. and often closed from 1 P.M. to 2 P.M. Some are closed on Thursday afternoon and all shut down on Sunday and legal holidays. Restaurants and nightspots are open until at least 1 A.M. and nightclubs normally keep their doors open until 3 A.M. Discotheques most certainly keep these hours.

ELECTRICITY. Throughout the island, the electricity is 110 volts, 60 cycles AC and appliances brought from North America are fine to use but those brought from the U.K. and Europe will need adapters.

MAIL, TELEPHONE, TELEGRAMS. Postal rates to the U.S. and Canada are 15 cents for airmail postcards, 20 cents per 10 grams for airmail letters. Jumbo postcards are also 20 cents. Rates to the U.K. are 15 cents for postcards, 25 cents for jumbo postcards and airmail letters per 10 grams. Direct distance dialing is available from Bermuda to the U.S., Canada, U.K., Northern Ireland, Australia, and parts of the West Indies. When dialing to Bermuda from these areas, the national number is: 809-(29). This code plus the required five-digit local number will reach your party. There is 24-hour cable service available and both night letter and direct full rates can apply.

USEFUL ADDRESSES. Airlines: *Air Canada,* 61 Front St., Hamilton. Tel: 3-2121; *American Airlines,* Chancery Lane, Hamilton. Tel: 3-1420; *British Airways,* 59 Front St., Hamilton. Tel: 5-4422; *Delta Airlines,* 56 Front St., Hamilton. Tel: 3-2000; *Eastern Airlines,* Front St., Hamilton. Tel: 2-5900.

Banks: *Bank of Bermuda,* Front St., Hamilton. Tel: 5-4000 (branches on Church St., Hamilton; St. George's; Somerset); *Bank of N.T. Butterfield & Son Ltd.,* Front St., Hamilton (branches in Somerset, St. George's and at Southampton Princess Hotel);

Bermuda Provident Bank Ltd., Church St., Hamilton.

GETTING AROUND. There are no self-drive cars for rent in Bermuda. Therefore, visitors have a choice of bicycles, buses, carriages, ferries, taxis or walking. Public transportation is excellent and both buses and ferries are a good way to get around. The more energetic may prefer motorbikes, the less active will want to take taxis everywhere.

By Cycle. Both pedal and motor-assisted bikes are available for rent at liveries throughout the island. It is illegal for anyone under 16 years of age to drive a motorbike, and all riders must, by law, wear safety helmets. Rental rates for motor-assisted cycles range from $11 to $18 per day plus deposit and insurance; pedal cycles run around $5 per day.

Gas stations are open from 7 A.M. to 7 P.M. Monday through Saturday only. Some are closed on Sunday and have restricted hours on public holidays.

By Bus. Bermuda's pink-and-blue buses are easy to spot, especially along the principal 24-mile route between Hamilton and St. George. Most buses operate every 15 minutes from early morning to late evening, Monday through Saturday. Bermuda is divided into 14 zones of about 2 miles each. Adult fares for traveling within the first 3 zones is 60 cents, and $1 for a longer ride. Bus Stops are green-and-white-striped posts, and passengers must have the correct change ready. It is not wise to be in too much of a hurry when you travel by bus. Between the speed limit and stops for passengers, it may take some time, but it's fun and a way to get to know the island at leisure. Listed below are some of the most popular destinations and what number bus to take there:

DESTINATION	ROUTE NUMBER
Aquarium	10, 11
Bermuda Museum	10, 11
Botanical Gardens	1, 2, 7
Belmont Hotel	8
Castle Harbour	1
Crystal Caves	3, 10, 11
Devil's Hole	1, 3
Dolphin Show	10, 11
Elbow Beach	2, 7
Gibbs Hill Lighthouse	7, 8

By Ferry. A wonderful way to travel from point to point. Take the Harbour Route between Hamilton, Paget and Warwick ($1), or try the Great Sound Route between Hamilton and Somerset Bridge ($2). Bicycles are also carried on ferries, the pedal kind are no charge but motorbikes cost $2.00 each, provided there is room on board (avoid rush hours) and one of the ship's mates will help you carry it on and off.

By Horse-Drawn Carriages. Still popular although their number has dwindled drastically in recent years. But you will find them lined up in the shade along Front Street in Hamilton, or in Flatt's Village. They are usually hired by the half-hour and 2 persons in a single carriage is about $7.50. 4 persons is about $10, and worth every romantic penny!

By Taxi. Taxi drivers in Bermuda provide more than transport. There are blue flags fluttering on the "bonnets" of 400 taxis on the island, signifying that the driver is a qualified tour guide. The men and women who earn the right to display the blue flag have passed both a written examination covering all facets of their island home and a practical test on courtesy, appearance, upkeep and driving ability. (In case you were curious, the question they are most frequently asked is why the water is so blue.) The drivers of these blue-flag taxis do not cost any more than other taxis and they will impart bits and pieces of information as you creep along at 20 mph (15 mph in town). There is even one driver who quotes Tom Moore's poetry in lilting Irish! Meter rates start at $1.60 for the first mile; each subsequent mile is 80¢, and there is a 25% surcharge between midnight and 6 A.M. Taxis can be hired by the hour or by the day for sightseeing at $11 per hour.

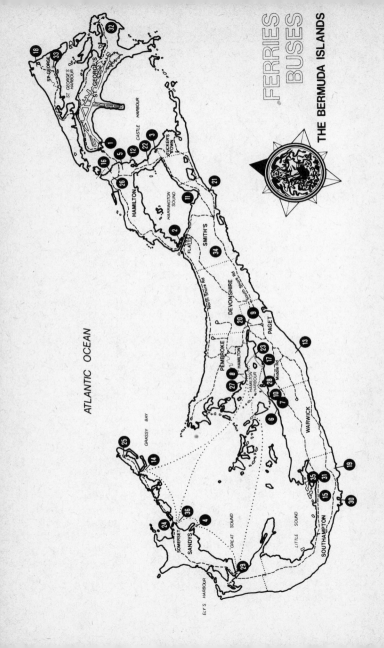

FERRIES
BUSES

THE BERMUDA ISLANDS

ATLANTIC OCEAN

BUS AND FERRY SCHEDULE

1 AIRPORT
2 AQUARIUM
3 CASTLE HARBOUR HOTEL
4 CAVELLO BAY—FERRY
5 CRYSTAL CAVES
6 BELMONT—FERRY
7 BELMONT HOTEL
8 BERMUDIANA HOTEL
9 BOTANICAL GARDENS
10 DARRELL'S WHARF—FERRY
11 DEVIL'S HOLE
12 DOLPHIN SHOW
13 ELBOW BEACH
14 FREEPORT—FERRY
15 GIBBS HILL LIGHTHOUSE
16 GROTTO BAY HOTEL
17 HODSDON'S FERRY
18 HOLIDAY INN
19 HORSESHOE BAY BEACH

20 HOSPITAL
21 JOHN SMITH'S BAY BEACH
22 LEAMINGTON CAVES
23 LOWER FERRY
24 MANGROVE BAY
25 MARITIME MUSEUM
26 PERFUME FACTORY
27 PRINCESS HOTEL
   (HAMILTON)
28 SALT KETTLE—FERRY
29 SOMERSET BRIDGE—FERRY
30 SONESTA BEACH HOTEL
31 SOUTHAMPTON PRINCESS
   HOTEL
32 ST. DAVID'S LIGHTHOUSE
33 TOWN OF ST. GEORGE
34 VERDMONT
35 WATERLOT INN
36 WATFORD BRIDGE—FERRY

HAMILTON/WARWICK Week days only (Fare $1 each way)

	a.m.	a.m.	a.m.	a.m.	a.m.	a.m.	a.m.	a.m.	noon	p.m.	p.m.
Lv. Hamilton	7.15	7.45	8.20	9.05	9.40	10.15	10.50	11.20	12.00	12.35	1.05
Lv. Lower Ferry	—	—	—	—	—	—	—	—	—	—	—
Lv. Hodsdon's	—	—	—	—	—	—	—	—	—	—	—
Lv. Salt Kettle	—	8.10	8.45	—	—	—	—	—	—	—	—
Lv Darrell's (Inverurie)	7.30	8.05	8.40	9.15	10.00	10.25	11.10	11.30	12.15	12.50	1.15
Lv. Belmont	—	7.55	8.30	9.20	9.50	10.30	11.00	11.35	12.10	12.45	1.20
Arr. Hamilton	7.40	8.15	8.50	9.30	10.10	10.40	11.20	11.45	12.25	1.00	1.30

Hamilton/Paget Week days only (Fare $1 each way)

	a.m.	a.m.	a.m.	a.m.	a.m.	a.m.	a.m.	a.m.	p.m.	p.m.	p.m.
Lv. Hemilton	8.10	8.40	8.55	9.30	10.00	10.35	11.05	11.35	12.10	12.45	1.15
Lv. Lower Ferry	8.15	8.45	9.00	9.50	10.05	10.55	11.10	11.55	12.15	1.05	1.20
Lv. Hodsdon's	8.20	8.50	9.05	9.45	10.10	10.50	11.15	11.50	12.20	1.00	1.25
Lv. Salt Kettle	8.25	—	9.10	9.40	10.15	10.45	11.20	11.45	12.25	12.55	1.30
Lv. Darrell's — (Inverurie)	—	—	—	—	—	—	—	12.30	—	—	—
Arr. Hamilton	8.30	8.55	9.15	9.55	10.20	11.00	11.25	12.00	12.40	1.10	1.35

Hamilton/Paget/Warwick Sundays only (Fare 2-50¢ pieces each way)

	a.m.	a.m.	a.m.	p.m.	p.m.	p.m.	p.m.	p.m.	p.m.	p.m.	p.m.	p.m.	p.m.
Lv. Hamilton	10.00	11.00	11.50	12.35	2.20	3.30	4.15	5.20	6.30	7.15	8.00	8.45	9.30
Lv. Lower Ferry	10.05	11.35	11.55	1.10	2.55	3.35	4.50	5.25	6.35	7.50	8.05	9.20	9.35
Lv. Hodsdon's	10.10	11.30	12.00	1.05	2.50	3.40	4.45	5.30	6.40	7.45	8.10	9.15	9.40
Lv. Salt Kettle	10.15	11.25	12.05	1.00	2.45	3.45	4.40	5.35	6.45	7.40	8.15	9.10	9.45
Lv. Darrell's (Inverurie)	10.20	11.20	12.10	12.55	2.40	3.50	4.35	5.40	6.50	7.35	8.20	9.05	9.50
Lv. Belmont	10.25	11.10	12.15	12.45	2.30	3.55	4.25	5.45	6.55	7.25	8.25	8.55	9.55
Arr. Hamilton	10.35	11.40	12.25	1.15	3.00	4.05	4.55	5.55	7.05	7.55	8.35	9.25	10.05

Note: [1] On Public Holidays Sunday Service will operate
[2]Timetable subject to change without notice.

(Please have American or Bermuda 50¢ coins available to operate turnstiles)

p.m.	p.m.	p.m.	p.m.	p.m.	p.m.	p.m.	p.m.	p.m.	p.m.	p.m.	p.m.	p.m.	p.m.	p.m.
1.40	2.30	3.20	4.05	4.35	5.10	5.40	6.20	7.05	7.40	8.30	9.10	10.00	10.40	11.20
—	—	—	—	—	—	5.45	6.25	7.35	7.45	9.00	9.15	10.30	10.45	11.50
—	—	—	—	—	—	5.50	6.30	7.30	7.50	8.55	9.20	10.25	10.50	11.45
—	—	—	—	—	—	5.55	6.35	7.25	7.55	8.50	9.25	10.20	10.55	11.40
1.55	2.40	3.35	4.15	4.50	5.20	6.00	6.40	7.20	8.00	8.45	9.30	10.15	11.00	11.35
1.50	2.45	3.30	4.20	4.45	5.25	6.05	6.45	7.15	8.05	8.40	9.35	10.10	11.05	11.30
2.05	2.55	3.45	4.30	5.00	5.35	6.15	6.55	7.40	8.15	9.05	9.45	10.35	11.15	11.55

(Please have American or Bermuda 50¢ coins available to operate turnstiles)

p.m.	p.m.	p.m.	p.m.	p.m.	p.m.	p.m.
1.45	2.10	2.45	3.30	4.15	4.55	5.20
2.05	2.15	3.05	3.35	4.35	5.00	5.25
2.00	2.20	3.00	3.40	4.30	5.05	5.30
1.55	2.25	2.55	3.45	4.25	5.10	5.35
—		—	—	—	—	5.45
2.10	2.30	3.10	3.50	4.40	5.15	5.55

Hamilton/Somerset (Fare $2 each way)

	Ex. Sun.	a.m.	a.m.	p.m.	p.m.	Sun Only	Ex. Sun.	Ex. Sun.
Lv. Hamilton	7.05	9.30	11.00	12.30	2.00	3.30	3.50	5.25
Lv. Freeport	7.30	—	—	—	—	—	4.50	
Lv. Watford	7.40	9.55	11.50	1.20	2.25	4.20	4.35	5.50
Lv. Cavello	7.50	10.05	11.40	1.10	2.35	4.10	4.25	6.00
Lv. Somerset Bridge	8.00	10.15	11.30	1.00	2.45	4.00	4.15	6.10
Arr. Hamilton	8.30	10.45	12.15	1.45	3.15	4.55	5.15	6.40

CRUISE TOURS: Bermuda Island Cruise—5 hours. Leaves Albuoy's Point, Hamilton at 11:00 A.M., Monday-Saturday. Cruise aboard *Pricilla, Maria* or *Susanna* (cap. 120-160 each), through the Great Sound, short stopover in Somerset for shopping. Includes picnic lunch and swimming, soft drinks, rum swizzles and Calypso entertainment. Approximately $25 per person. Operated by Kitson & Co. Ltd. (American Sightseeing), tel: 5-2525.

Sea Garden Cruise (February-December)—2 hours. Leaves Ferry Terminal, Hamilton at 10:00 A.M. and 2:00 P.M., Monday-Saturday. Cruise through Great Sound to coral reefs aboard glass bottom boat, *Reef Explorer* (cap. 50). Commentary by experienced cruise director. Approximately $10 per person. Operated by Kitson & Co. Ltd. (American Sightseeing), tel: 5-2525.

Sea Garden, Snorkeling Cruise (late May-early November)—4 hours. Leaves Robinson's Marina, Somerset Bridge at 9:50 A.M. and 1:50 P.M. daily. Cruise 5 miles northwest to "The Perimeter Reef" to see shipwrecks and marine life by glass bottom boat (cap. 25). Snorkeling equipment free, instruction if required. Approximately $20 per person. Operated by Pitman's Boat Tours, tel: 4-0700.

Catamaran Cruise (April-November)—3 hours. Leaves Ferry Terminal, Hamilton at 10:15 A.M. and 2:00 P.M., Monday-Saturday. Rum punch cruise aboard 2 hulled Catamaran (cap. 40), through Great Sound to various islands for sailing, snorkeling, swimming, and sunbathing. Commentary by experienced cruise director. Includes all equipment. Approximately $15 per person. Operated by Halcolm Lightbourne, tel: 1-4261/1-5023.

Moonlight Fun Cruise (begins in June)—2½ hours. Leave Albuoy's Point, Hamilton and cruise through Great Sound in *Gay Venture*. Dancing, games, limbo, sing-a-long, swizzles, and prizes. Approximately $12 per person. Operated by Kitson & Co. Ltd., tel: 5-2525.

Scenic Sea Gardens Cruise—3 hours. Leaves Ferry Terminal, Hamilton, Monday to Sunday at 9:45 A.M. Cruise aboard glass bottom boat *Defiance* (cap. 150), 2 viewing decks and a sun deck. Rum swizzles and beer served. Approximately $14 per person. Operated by Kitson & Co. Ltd., tel: 5-2525.

Cruise and Glass Bottom Boat Trip—2 hours. Leaves Williams Marine at 10:00 A.M. and 2:00 P.M., Monday-Saturday. Cruise to sea gardens then transfer to glass bottom boat (cap. 15). Covers 15 miles. Commentary by Bermudian Skipper. Approximately $10 per person. Operated by Williams Marine Ltd., tel: 5-3727.

Combination Cruise and Sea Gardens Visit—3 hours. Leaves Williams Marine at 10:00 A.M. and 2:00 P.M., Monday-Saturday. Covers 22 miles at western end. Stop at sea gardens. Commentary by Bermudian skipper and includes Coke or Pirates Punch. Approximately $14 per person. Operated by Williams Marine Ltd., tel: 5-3727.

Scenic Cruise Deluxe "Encore"—5½ hours. Leaves Williams Marine at 10:30 A.M., Monday-Saturday. Cruise around the western end of Bermuda, stopover at sea gardens. Tour Bermuda Maritime Museum in Dockyard and then enjoy a buffet lunch there. Rum punch served on cruise. Approximately $25 per person. Operated by Williams Marine Ltd., tel: 5-3727.

Sailing Cruise (June-October)—5½ hour trip. 10:15 A.M., Tuesday and Thursday only—$30 per person includes lunch and drinks.

3 hour trip—10:15 A.M. and 2:15 P.M., Wednesday and Friday only—$17 per person. Leaves Williams Marine and sail aboard 40-foot ketch *Alibi* through Great Sound. Includes rum punch and soft drinks. Operated by Williams Marine Ltd., tel: 5-3727.

Cocktail Cruise—1½ hours. Tuesday, Thursday and Saturday evenings only. Leaves Williams Marine 5:30 P.M. for cruise around Hamilton Harbour. Including drinks, $10 per person. Operated by Williams Marine Ltd., tel: 5-3727.

Moonlight Cruise—2½ hours. Tuesday, Thursday and Saturday during summer season only. Leaves Albuoy's Point, Hamilton at 9:45 P.M. for cruise through Great Sound. Returns at 12:15 A.M. Bar facilities and dancing. $12 per person, including one drink. Operated by Kitson & Co. Ltd. (American Sightseeing), tel: 5-2525.

Bus Tours (March 1 to November 30): Combination St. George's/Harrington Sound—5 hours. This tour leaves Hamilton about 10:00 A.M., Monday-Saturday. Visits the caves, aquarium, museum, Devil's Hole, perfume factory and town of St. George. Includes admissions and lunch. Approximately $25 per person. Can be booked through: Gutteridge, Kitson, Penboss, Butterfield.

Harrington Sound Tour (groups only)—3 hours. This tour operates Monday-Saturday and includes admissions to the caves, aquarium, Devil's Hole and perfume factory. Approximately $16 per person. Can be booked through Penboss.

Taxi Tours: Harrington Sound Tour—3 hours. Visits to aquarium and museum, Devil's Hole, the caves and perfume factory. Includes admissions only. Can be booked through: Butterfield,

$16–18—4 per cab; Kitson, $20–22—3 per cab; Penboss $25–30—2 per cab; Gutteridge, rates available on request.

Hamilton Tour From Holiday Inn—5 hours. Tour of tourist attractions along the route from Holiday Inn to Hamilton. Includes admissions and lunch. Book through Gutteridge, rates available on request.

Harrington Sound St. George's—5 hours. Visits to aquarium and museum, Devil's Hole, the caves, perfume factory and town of St. George. Includes admissions only. Book through Butterfield or Penboss, $20–24—4 per cab; $25–30—3 per cab; $35–42.50—2 per cab.

Somerset Tour—4 hours. Visits to Gibbs Hill Lighthouse, St. James Church, Cedar Souvenir Shop, Cambridge Beaches and Linen Shop. Includes admissions and lunch in Somerset. Book through Penboss, $30 per person, 2 per cab.

St. George's Tour—5 hours. Tour of St. George's with guide. Includes admissions to the caves, Devil's Hole, aquarium and museum and perfume factory and lunch. Book through Gutteridge, rates available on request.

Nightclub Tour (groups only). Tour includes cover charge into one of Bermuda's popular nightclubs, 2 drinks and gratuities. Book through Gutteridge or Kitson, rates available on request.

SHOPPING. There are some excellent buys in Bermuda, such as English bone china, Irish linens, Scottish tweeds and cashmere sweaters, and liquor. There are some local handicrafts, pottery, cedar ware, and paintings by local artists. Sports gear, cameras, watches, and resort wear can also be found. Most shops take credit cards and some stores will open up a charge account in your name.

CLUBS AND ORGANIZATIONS. There are international service clubs and organizations, benevolent and patriotic associations, lodges, special-interest and sporting organizations in Bermuda. Visitors can attend the local *Kiwanis* or *Rotary*, *Elks* or *Freemasons*, *AA*, *Confrerie des Chevaliers du Tastevin*, or get a letter of introduction to the *Royal Bermuda Yacht Club*. For a full list of local clubs and organizations, check with any office of the Bermuda Department of Tourism. For addresses in Bermuda, check with the telephone directory.

CUSTOMS ON DEPARTURE. All passengers departing for the U.S. by air will clear U.S. Customs at the Bermuda Airport. These passengers must complete the U.S. Customs declaration and, following check-in and seat assignment from the carrier, pass through the Customs area. Under a recent change in law, U.S. citizens may now take back $300 of merchandise duty-free, after 48 hours and once every 30 days. **Canadians** may take back $50 of merchandise duty-free after 48 hours and once every three calendar months, or $150 after 7 days once every calendar year. **U.K.** citizens may take back £ 10 worth of goods, duty-free.

Note: U.S. citizens should check their state's liquor and tobacco import regulations before coming to Bermuda.

 DEPARTURE TAX. Air passengers departing Bermuda must pay $5 at the time of airport check-in. The port tax for ship passengers is $20, collected in advance by the steamship company. Children under 2 years of age are exempt from all taxes.

BERMUDA'S PAST AND PRESENT

Pink Houses and Purple Onions

Blessed with a beautiful landscape and surrounded by a turquoise sea, Britain's oldest colony and most famous resort island lies isolated in the Atlantic Ocean, more than 500 miles from the nearest land (Cape Hatteras, North Carolina). The 55,000 residents of these lovely islands live on some 21-square miles of land atop a subterranean mountain, and are known affectionately as "onions" after the sweet, succulent Bermuda onion that was their livelihood a century ago. But they are also known for Bermuda shorts, the Bermuda Fitted Dinghy, Easter lilies, and limestone houses with "icing-on-the-cake" roofs that sparkle in the sun. These distinctive homes are all lovingly painted in pastel colors and known by their given names, rather than by numbers.

On one of his many holiday excursions to the island between 1867 and his death in 1910, Mark Twain is supposed to have said, "Bermuda is Heaven but you have to go through Hell to get there!" Today's 11,000 or so weekly visitors to Bermuda will find the remarks of the American humorist only half right. It is still a "heavenly" place but one can now get there with the greatest of ease. It is less than a two-hour flight from the East Coast, nonstop across the Atlantic from London, and a leisurely 36 hours from New York by luxury cruise vessel.

Some Early Visitors

Bermuda has welcomed travellers with open arms for over three centuries. In fact, one might say that Sir George Somers and his shipwrecked party of 150 who landed in 1609 were the first visitors. They remained at the eastern end of the island (St. George's) only long enough to build two new vessels and gather provisions to continue their journey to the Jamestown Settlement in Virginia. And when they sailed away nine and a half months later, they sang such praises of the place that word reached the Virginia Company in London, which financed the first group of settlers two years later. The story of their adventure also reached William Shakespeare and it inspired his last play, *The Tempest.* Another early "tourist" was an ailing clergyman from Massachusetts who spent seven months in Bermuda in 1663 and returned home so rejuvenated that he outlived three wives, fathering a brood of children along the way!

One of the colony's most endearing visitors was an Irish poet named Tom Moore who spent the first four months of 1804 in St. George working in the court and writing romantic verse in his spare time. One of the many stories still told about Moore is his amorous attachment to a neighbor's wife and many persist in believing that the "Nea" in his poems refer to this woman, Hester Tucker, and that her first born is described as "the first ambrosial childe of bliss." More to fact is the time Moore did spend at "Walsingham," the beautiful 17th-century home of Samuel Trott and his family where he immortalized the calabash tree in the front yard. The gnarled tree is still there and the old house became Tom Moore's Tavern about 75 years ago. It is located just off Harrington Sound Road in Hamilton Parish and is a delightful place to visit for local seafood and a Tom Moore special punch. The paneled walls and the archways on the front porch are just as they were when the poet visited.

Haven for High Society

But many Bermudians feel that tourism as a serious business began in the winter of 1883 with the arrival of Princess Louise, daughter of Queen Victoria, who fled the cold and wintry climate of Canada where her husband was the governor-general. The residents of this crown colony had never seen a real-live princess and, no doubt, her visit did receive much attention in the press of the English-speaking world. It also inspired the opening of the colony's first hotel, the Princess Hotel in Hamilton, which provided all the amenities the rich and playful needed including direct telephones to the city. This was the beginning of a trend that would last until World War II. During the winter months, the wealthy began to come to Bermuda for "the season," together with their ladies' maids and steamer trunks full of tea-dance dresses. They drank lots of tea, played croquet or tennis and visited their friends via horse-drawn carriage. Tennis was *le sport* and came to Bermuda as early as 1873 and the first tennis tournament in the Western Hemisphere took place here in 1877. (A young Bermudian lady, Miss Mary Outerbridge, introduced the game to the United States in 1874 by taking her equipment and book of rules to the Staten Island Cricket Club in New York.)

Soon, larger and newer hotels sprang up around the island and the "guest house" concept was born. Many visitors then (and now) wouldn't stay in anything else because they said this captures "the real" Bermuda. In the 1920s, the exclusive Mid-Ocean Club in Tucker's Town was founded, with a golf course that equaled any in the world, and golf became *le sport*.

Bermuda was especially popular during the roaring '20s because it was still quaint but civilized and alcohol was legal. During the Prohibition years in the U.S., those that could afford it did their drinking aboard steamships back and forth to the island. The first commercial passenger flights between New York and Bermuda were offered in the late '30s while as many as six different steamship lines scheduled weekly sailings. As the island's popularity as a resort increased, visitors arrived year-round, not just for "the season," to fill the hotels, cottages and guest houses and travel about by the new narrow gauge railway between Hamilton and St. George's that was as undependable as it was charming.

A New Era

But alas, with the advent of World War II, the large cruise vessels in Hamilton harbor were painted a dull gray and sent on more somber missions. Bermuda lost the "beautiful people" for a few years but the slack was taken up with British and American forces. The U.S. was given a 99-year lease on a square mile of land that surrounds the airport and brought motorized vehicles to ruin the roads. Through it all, the colony hung tenaciously to her charm, and the tourists flocked back after the war as fast as they had fled.

Today, the island receives over half a million visitors a year who come to play golf or tennis out the back door of large resort hotels, lounge around cottage colonies and beaches, stay in small guest houses, or take housekeeping apartments with their families. Bermuda has subtly adapted to her visitors and now offers something for everyone. While honeymooners may pick the traditional months of June or September, couples come anytime to celebrate their anniversaries. Golfers may be wooed during the winter months but the greens and fairways are inviting year-round. And there is plenty to do to keep the whole family busy. After a morning at the beach, young ones can visit maritime and historical museums, dolphins that dance, underground caves, and have a tug of war with a turtle. It all costs money but the beautiful beaches are still free.

Traditions

Bermudians treasure their traditions and like to share them with visitors—both the colonial pomp they have inherited and the local ceremonies they developed. The justices still wear powdered wigs as they impart British law but can be found on the evening circuit in Bermuda shorts. The crown-appointed governor appears in full plumage on special occasions. He journeys to St. George every spring to collect the annual rent for the old State House of one peppercorn (presented on a velvet pillow), throws a garden party in June to celebrate the queen's official birthday, and hitches up a pair of fine horses to the state landau to open Parliament in the fall. (The

present governor is the Hon. Sir Richard Posnett.)

Christmastime in Bermuda traditionally means passing around the cassava pie, made from a recipe handed down for 300 years, and running out to join the Gombey Dancers who wend their way along the narrow lanes on Boxing Day (December 26). The local wedding tradition features a horse-drawn carriage for the bride and groom and separate wedding cakes. The groom has a single layer covered with gold leaf while the bride cuts a three-tiered silver cake topped with a cedar sapling. This custom, adapted from the Dutch, dictates that the couple plant the sapling on their wedding day (hopefully in front of their new home) and if it grows straight and strong, so will their marriage. Sports are another local tradition and Bermudians all flock to the beaches on Bermuda Day (May 24), the official opening of the swimming season. Sailing, soccer and cricket are favorite pastimes and the annual Cup Match between the island's two cricket teams is an official holiday.

Bermuda Shorts

As reflected by their dress, Bermudians live a casual life that has a tinge of quiet elegance to it. During the winter months, men wear tartans, light tweeds, and pullovers and from May to November, the famous Bermuda shorts are de rigueur. Shorts that stopped just above the knee and worn with long socks that were turned over just below the knee were introduced to the island in the early 1900s by members of the British military. The early styles were dull gray and khaki, belted and baggy, but they kept the troops cool in the midday sun.

By the 1920s, tailors along Front Street were making streamlined versions and local Hamilton merchants were wearing the shorts, along with knee socks, tie and jacket, during the working day but never to dinner or church (!). Bermuda shorts were born. But there were always strict rules—the proper length was two to four inches above the knees, and there was a time in the 1950s when local police handed out "green tickets" to wearers of shorts that were "too short." Although the official Bermuda short season for the police force is May to November, many local gentlemen wear them year-round. They even wear them with evening dress in the summer and abroad in the middle of winter. It has become their trademark!

Architecture

Bermuda has its own style of architecture that was developed as early as 1620 when Governor Moore ordered the building of a proper

State House. Because wooden structures with raffia roofs did not withstand the ravages of storms, Moore ordered a simple and functional building of native stone with thick walls, low ceilings, and a flat roof. The flat roof was the governor's only error. Not only did it always leak, it couldn't catch the precious rain which was the island's only source of pure water. Bermudians have wisely emulated their ancestors' functional design and it is this uniformity of construction with stone walls and stepped roofs that make for a unique style. Highly polished cedar doors and floors, large fireplaces that served a double purpose (cooking and heating), and "tray" ceilings have been an integral part of the Bermudian home for three centuries.

These buildings were all made of native Bermudian coral, an aeolian limestone quarried by hand and cut into rectangular blocks, then plastered on both sides to prevent deterioration. When put into place, the blocks were given several coats of whitewash. These blocks were actually quarried from the backyard of the newly designated structure, and the excavation was utilized as a storage tank for fresh water. The building's roof of limestone slabs was pitched so rain water could be channeled down through stone gutters to the storage tank. Still practiced today, modern tanks are underground with flat roofs of reinforced concrete. To keep the rain water fresh and pure, a lime wash was applied regularly to the roof (a nontoxic white paint is now used). It is this "icing-on-the-cake" roof that is so distinctively Bermudian. Modern houses are now also built of cement block and stucco but the construction is the same. Over the years, their exterior walls have been painted bright Bermuda pink, pumpkin orange, pastel blue, green or yellow.

Inside, native cedar has been used for centuries for the beams, floors, furniture, door and window frames. This cedar, now practically extinct from a blight of the 1940s, adapts well to woodworking, adds a special warmth to the structure, and lasts forever (the early colonists used this cedar for shipbuilding). Other charming features of a typical Bermudian home were the "welcoming arms" stairway to the front door (built wider at the bottom than at the top to welcome you), and the "tray" ceilings devised to counteract the extreme height of the roof and collect heat from the rooms. As the term suggests, the ceilings are shaped like the inside of an upside down tea tray.

Some of the older homes still have a separate buttery, or ice house, a miniature of the larger building but topped with a decorative sphere on its roof. "Slave walls," or dry stone walls built by former slaves, are also apparent. Bermudians treated their slaves well and rarely traded them once they became part of the family. They housed them either in the basement of the family home or in a dwelling of their own on the same property.

Every spring sometime between mid-March and mid-May, private Bermudian homes and gardens are open to the public during an annual tour sponsored by the Garden Club of Bermuda. A different set of three homes is open each Wednesday over a four-week period and the properties chosen are large and small, with a good cross-section of the new and old. Visitors on the tour will be impressed that Bermuda houses do not have numbers but names lovingly bestowed like Open Hearth, Orange Grove, Cedar Hill, Salt Winds and Heron's Nest.

At least two historic houses are open to visitors year-round. The 17th-century mansion Verdmont (Collector's Hill, Smith's Parish) was built between 1616 and 1662 by Captain William Sayle, twice governor of the island. The cedar staircase in the house is considered to be the finest in Bermuda, and the windows still have most of their original panes.

The Tucker House (Water Street, St. George's) was the home of Henry Tucker whose father, Colonel Tucker of Southampton, led the conspiracy to give gunpowder to the American colonies in exchange for food, and is a fine example of a mid-18th-century house. It is full of beautiful, old family furniture, much of it presented by Robert Tucker of Baltimore (who lived to be 102!). Some of the Tucker sons were educated at William and Mary College and remained in the United States. A Thomas Tudor Tucker, brother of Henry, became a treasurer of the U.S.

Gombey Dancers

A local Christmas season tradition is the appearance of the Gombey dancers on Boxing Day (December 26) and they sing and dance their way around the island like pied pipers, bringing many of the children along with them in a carnival-like atmosphere. The Gombeys emerged during the slavery days in Bermuda, with music and rhythm brought from Africa and the West Indies. The word "gombey" means rhythm or the skin-covered drum the original dancers used. In the Bahamas, the word is "Goombay" and a native Jamaican dance is known as a "Gumby."

The dancers wear colorful costumes with beads, sequins, fringe and tassels. They wear high headdresses topped with feathers and covered with tiny mirrors that reflect and distort the scenes around them as they move. Grotesque masks enhance their frenzied, winding movement and coins are traditionally thrown at their feet to make them move faster. They are accompanied only by drummers who play simply by ear and instinct. Most of them do not read music.

Gombey dancing is a Christmas custom as important as the evergreen trees imported from North America, the poinsettias blooming wild all over the island, and cassava pie. This is made from a 300-year-old recipe that calls for spiced cassava dough and a filling of beef, pork and chicken.

Geography

Bermuda is a tiny dot on any world map, remote from the nearest land. There are about 150 islands, the seven largest connected by bridges and causeways and arranged in the shape of a giant fish hook. From east to west, Bermuda is about 22 miles long with a maximum width of less than two miles, forming a land area of 20.59 square miles. Geologists say that this land area is perched on the summit of a submarine mountain that rises 15,000 feet from the bottom of the sea, and was created some 100 million years ago by a volcano. The islands are surrounded by coral reefs that have protected them from unwanted invaders as well as natural erosion.

Bermuda has a mild, subtropical climate because the Gulf Stream tempers the wintry winds that sweep across the Atlantic from west and north. The average yearly temperature is 70 degrees F. (21

degrees C.) and annual rainfall is 1,270 mm (50 inches), spread evenly over the 12 months. The sun shines an average of seven hours per day, 351 days a year. However, because Bermuda is entirely surrounded by water, the variables in any given day can range from intense solar heat to cool, gusty winds and heavy rain squalls. (The visitor must be prepared for anything!)

Winters, cooler than in the Caribbean, are a time for active sports such as golf or tennis. Spring comes early to the island, along with oleander, hibiscus and bougainvillea that bloom along every roadside. The days are warm and sunny from late spring through early fall, and water sports prevail as favorite pastimes for both residents and visitors. This is truly the Land of Water.

Early History

Credit for discovery of the islands in 1503 is given to Spanish navigator Juan de Bermudez who gave the area his name. A map published in the *Legatio Babylonica* in 1511 includes an island called "La Bermuda." But the Spanish never attempted to settle the area in the 16th century and referred to it as "Isles of the Devils" and said that it was inhabited by bad spirits who lured ships to their graveyard among the treacherous reefs. Another historical source says that in 1515, a Gonzales Ferdinando d'Oviedo tried to land pigs on the islands to provide food for the crews of ships that came near or were wrecked along the reefs.

So Bermuda was uninhabited when 150 passengers aboard the

300-ton *Sea Venture* were shipwrecked off what is now St. Catherine's Beach and spent almost a year on the eastern end of the island between 1609 and 1610. The *Sea Venture* was the flagship of a nine vessel fleet that set sail from Plymouth, England on June 2, 1609 to carry colonists and provisions to the new Jamestown Settlement in Virginia. Among the prominent passengers on board sent by the Jamestown Company were: Sir George Somers, Admiral of the fleet; Sir Thomas Gates, deputy governor of Jamestown; his aide, William Strachey; and John Rolfe, who later married the Indian Princess Pocahontas and made American history books.

After almost two months at sea, the *Sea Venture* ran into a hurricane that threw her off course from the rest of the fleet. For three days the vessel tossed, filling with water. Just as the passengers had given up hope of keeping her afloat, land was sighted. Sir George ordered the vessel landward but she ran aground on a reef at the eastern end of Bermuda. Through the wisdom of their two leaders, all 150 passengers and most of their provisions were landed safely in small boats on the beach below St. Catherine's Point.

During a stay of nine and a half months on the island, the men of the party built two new ships, the *Deliverance* and *Patience*, from the salvaged wreck of the *Sea Venture* and the tall, strong cedars they found, while the women gathered food. By the second week in May 1610, the castaways were prepared to continue their journey and sailed for Jamestown, leaving two men behind by their own preference. One was a convicted murderer and the other, Christopher Carter, is frequently called Bermuda's first settler.

Sir George and his party arrived in Jamestown within two weeks and found the small settlement sick and starving. He offered to return to Bermuda for more food, and there he died of exhaustion. His nephew, Matthew Somers, buried the heart of Sir George near their original landing site of 1609 and carried the body back to England aboard the *Patience* (disregarding the needs of Jamestown).

Soon, fascinating tales of the "Somers Islands" were the talk of London and the Virginia Company. A letter describing the adventure in detail was sent from Jamestown by William Strachey to the Countess of Bedford, who shared it with members of the Virginia Company. These included the Earl of Southampton, a patron of William Shakespeare who based his last and most idyllic play *The Tempest* on the Bermuda happening.

Two years later, some fifty-odd settlers, sponsored by the Virginia Company, sailed into the harbor at the eastern end of Bermuda and founded the town of St. George, in honor of Sir George Somers and St. George, the patron saint of England. (It became the capital of Bermuda for 203 years.) By 1616, the whole 21 miles of square land was surveyed and divided into eight large tribes, each one named after a member of the company (now called the Bermuda Company), and bounded by a path just wide enough to roll a barrel along. These tribes are the parishes we know today and the tribe roads are still in existence. (The parishes are Sandys, Southampton, Warwick, Paget, Pembroke, Devonshire, Smith's, Hamilton, and St. George's, which makes the ninth.)

In 1620, the newly appointed Governor Butler convened Bermuda's first Parliament in St. Peter's Church (the site of the oldest Anglican church in the Western Hemisphere in continuous use) and set about building a proper State House. His foresight in constructing the building entirely of native limestone, to withstand the ravages of storms as well as to save the already dwindling supply of indigenous cedar, set the example for traditional Bermudian architecture. The State House is Bermuda's oldest building but has not been in official use since the capital moved to Hamilton in 1815. (It is in trust to the Masonic Lodge for an annual rent of one peppercorn which is paid in a colorful ceremony every April.)

Toward the end of the 17th century, Bermuda officially became a Crown Colony, governed by the British monarch. The islanders supported themselves through shipbuilding with native cedar, trading salt from the Turks Islands, slaves from Africa and the West Indies, whaling and privateering. Of all these trades, piracy was the most lucrative and on the sea Bermudians were a tough lot to surpass. The coffers of St. George were full of foreign coins either from far-flung sailings or from the ships wrecked along the island reefs. They got so rich from piracy that agriculture was neglected and the islands were soon dependent upon their American cousins for most of their food supply. They bartered food for salt brought up from the Turks Islands.

Ties that Bind

The link that was established between the Bermuda Islands, American colonies and Great Britain in 1609 grew stronger during the early history of both colonies and, indeed, has never been broken. When the "shot heard 'round the world" was fired on the village green in Concord, Massachusetts in 1775, the Bermudians attempted to remain neutral, considering the confrontation between their American cousins and the Mother Country a private spat. But soon the islanders were bitterly divided over the American Revolu-

tion because many of them had families and close connections in the colonies, especially Virginia. While the Bermudians as a whole had no intention of cutting their ties with the Mother Country, they realized that they had to be at peace with the Americans or they faced starvation.

In the summer of 1775, Colonel Henry Tucker (whose son was a student at William and Mary College in Williamsburg, Virginia) appeared before the Continental Congress to plead for the continuation of trading salt for food, but the Americans turned down the request because they wanted gunpowder. Informed that a large stock of gunpowder was stored on the island, General Washington wrote to the citizens of Bermuda from his camp outside Boston, begging them to sell the gunpowder to his army in exchange for a continuation of friendship and provisions. However, before his letter even had time to reach the island, a small group of Bermudians took matters into their own hands. In the heat of a mid-August night, they removed the entire store of gunpowder and relayed it to two American warships anchored outside St. George's harbor. (The names of those involved are still spoken in whispers but there is no doubt that the Tucker family was behind the scheme.) Although the governor was furious when he found out, Bermuda continued to be supplied with food throughout the war.

During the War of 1812, Bermuda became an active base for the Royal Navy and her fine harbors a repository for captured American warships. *The President*, one of the vessels brought in, was the victim of the last sea battle in January 1815. Aboard *The President* was a young seaman named Richard Sutherland Dale. He was wounded and soon died. He was buried in St. Peter's graveyard and his tombstone is inscribed with the gratitude of his parents for the tender care he received from the citizens of St. George's.

Slavery was abolished in Bermuda in 1834 but most of the island favored the southern Confederacy during the American Civil War, especially the area around St. George. Blockade running was the name of the game during this war, and the warehouses of St. George were soon full of guns for the Confederate Army and cotton bound for Europe. But fast riches did not last and by 1865, the end of the war, the townsfolk were in debt with unsold rotten goods in the warehouses.

But one can still find the remnants of this brief glory. The Confederate Museum, in the very building where much of the wartime operations took place, is full of memorabilia of the ''gilded'' days of the 1860s. Local residents will also point out Barber's Alley, which adjoins the kitchen of the Tucker home where a former South Carolina slave named Joseph Hayes Rainey set up a barber shop. He and his wife fled to Bermuda prior to the Civil War but returned to South Carolina in 1865 where he became the first black elected to the U.S. House of Representatives.

Spy Story

During World War II, the colony played her most fascinating role. The story is best told in William Stevenson's *A Man Called Intrepid*, an exciting account of the secret diplomacy and intelligence operations of the allied powers. According to Stevenson, there were some 1,200 British experts working in the cellars of the pink Hamilton Princess Hotel, intercepting mail and messages between the United States and the Continent. These men and women, recruited in England, were trained to decipher microdot messages sent by German spies in ordinary letters. Most of the messages were in mail carried on the New York/Europe route which landed in Bermuda ''to refuel.'' While passengers and crew were treated to tea, the experts could examine and reseal as many as 200,000 pieces of mail and cargo per plane. Stevenson reports that the majority of these ''trappers'' were MI-5 women with ''long ears, sharp eyes, and well-turned ankles.'' For some reason, the prettier the ankle, the better a woman was at the job of detection.

In addition to exposing German spies in the U.S., the trappers saved a collection of 270 Impressionist paintings stolen by the Nazis in France. The paintings were taken off a ship in Bermuda harbor, stored in a local bank vault, and returned to their (astonished!) rightful owner at the end of the war. Tracking enemy U-boats was another activity on the island and a German submarine became a secret prize of the war—and put into immediate use as a training vessel for both the Royal and U.S. navies.

During World War II, Prime Minister Winston Churchill made one of several visits to Bermuda—this one in earnest. He flew in and out in January 1942 on a Pan Am Clipper and addressed the Bermuda Assembly in between. He was so impressed with the atmosphere on the island that in 1953, he suggested the Big Three hold their summit meeting at the Mid-Ocean Club and Eisenhower, Churchill and French Premier Laniel gathered. Eisenhower returned in 1957 to confer with Prime Minister Macmillan. In 1961, Macmillan joined with President Kennedy for the Bermuda Conference, and President Nixon and Prime Minister Edward Heath met there in 1971.

After almost 200 years in Bermuda, the British withdrew their forces in 1957 but the U.S. Naval Air Stations continue at Kindley Field until the year 2040, according to the rent-free lease. In addition, one of the most important stations in the space-tracking network of the National Aeronautics and Space Administration operates on Cooper's Island at Bermuda's eastern end. Locally, Bermuda has her own army, the Bermuda regiment with a strength of approximately 450 part-time soldiers.

Government

Bermuda has been a Crown Colony since 1684 and her constitution remained relatively unchanged until 1968 when Bermudians were given a greater say in the conduct of local affairs, superseding the constitution of 1888. The Bermuda government is composed of a crown-appointed governor, a premier and his cabinet, the House of Assembly and the Legislative Council.

The Cabinet: This body of 12 is headed by the premier, a person appointed by the governor as the one most likely to command the confidence of the majority of the House of Assembly. Each member of the Cabinet is appointed by the governor, acting on the advice of the premier, and assigned an area of government operation. There is, for example, a minister of health and welfare as well as ministers of tourism, transportation, agriculture, immigration and education.

House of Assembly: The five-year elected body of government is composed of 40 "mp's" or Members of Parliament. The island is

divided into 20 electoral districts, four for Pembroke Parish and two for each of the other eight parishes. The ruling political party is the United Bermuda Party while the opposition is called the Progressive Labor Party. The election of 1968 was the first held in Bermuda under a party system, and the first in which all registered voters over the age of 21 were eligible to cast a ballot.

The Senate: Also known as the upper house of Parliament. There are 11 members of the Senate who must approve bills before the governor signs them into statute. Four of the members are appointed on the advice of the premier, two on the advice of the opposition leader and five by the governor himself.

Judicial responsibility falls to the Supreme Court, which is headed by a crown-appointed chief justice. (The present chief justice appointed by Queen Elizabeth is a distinguished black Bermudian.) The judges impart English law in traditional robes and wigs. There is also an appeal court and two lower courts.

Economics

In the absence of nearly all forms of direct taxation, the government of Bermuda obtains most of its revenues from the duty on all imported goods for visitors and residents. There is no local income tax but a small land tax was instituted in 1967 to increase revenue. Visitors will also find a 5 percent room tax and one of the highest airport taxes in the world ($5 per person). Port taxes for cruise passengers are also very steep.

There is no doubt that the people of Bermuda enjoy a high standard of living, with no personal income tax, practically no unemployment, and no national debt. But the cost of living is also high even though the government has managed to keep inflation to a modest 3 percent. A home can sell for as high as $3 million (a nonBermudian may not purchase one for less than $300,000), a small dresser for the bedroom can run up to $700 after import duties, and a dozen eggs sell for about $2 in the local supermarket.

There is no heavy industry in Bermuda, and the economy is now based on tourism and on companies that set up headquarters on the island to avoid heavy taxation and complicated laws at home. These British, American, and Canadian companies pay some form of taxation to the Bermuda government but are "exempt" from others. Some of them are no more than a file in a drawer but others, like Bacardi International, have built an elegant headquarters and hired many local residents. But 65 cents of every dollar spent in Bermuda comes via tourism.

The economic turn to tourism, which came with the steamships of the early 1900s, has been a fortuitous one. There are now over 100 hotels, cottage colonies, housekeeping apartments and guest houses. However, tourism is heavily controlled by the government, with laws designed to save local jobs (should the market fall) as well

as preserve tourist facilities. There has been a moratorium on building new hotels or even adding to ones that are not owned by Bermudians. Only certain wholesalers are allowed to package vacation programs in Bermuda, only scheduled aircraft are allowed to bring in visitors, and only a certain number of cruise vessels can dock at any given time. The opening up of St. George as a regular cruise call has given accessibility to the eastern end of the island, spreading visitors about more evenly and preventing overcrowding of facilities.

But visitors will only return again and again as long as there are no internal problems. The question of independence is debated with one faction for, the other against. Loyalists argue that the island doesn't need it and can't afford it. But some fear that Great Britain may prefer it. However, there are other problems that are much more important to the colony's 55,000 people, of whom approximately 30,000 are black.

In the spring of 1973, Governor Richard Christopher Sharples and his aide were assassinated while taking an evening stroll on the grounds of Government House. It was a shot that rocked the island's small world. In the fall of 1977, the convicted assassins were hung until dead, and this deed rocked certain parts of the black community. Riots caused millions of dollars in destruction and kept residents inside during strict curfew hours. Thousands of potential visitors stayed away and hotels (asked to keep open by the government as a vote of confidence) suffered enormous losses. However, the beauty of Bermuda soon lured the tourists back again and all was well, at least on the surface.

"Whither the Fates lead us" (Quo Fata Ferunt) has been the motto of Bermudians since 1615 and the fates have done well by them so far. There is no doubt that with all Bermudians working together, this beautiful island will remain steady despite an unsteady world.

EXPLORING BERMUDA

Clean Air, Crystal Water and Fragrant Flowers

Exploring the 21 square miles of this beautiful island in the Atlantic is a treat in breathtaking views of the sea and shore and colorful, subtropical flowers and plants that grace every byway. Oleander and hibiscus hedges dominate the scenery while palm trees and cacti provide a lush background. On some of the narrower lanes, the flora is so prolific that it almost forms a ceiling for you to pass under. Indeed, a sunny day in Bermuda is meant for chugging along the charming roads of the island, breathing in the fresh and fragrant air.

The best way to explore Bermuda is via Mopeds or, as the Bermudians say, motor-assisted cycles. These are for rent everywhere at cycle liveries by the hour, the day, the week or longer. Both single cycles and two-seaters are available and very safe, providing you obey the speed limit, wear the proper clothing and your safety helmet at all times. As the air is clean and pure, there is no danger of breathing unhealthy fumes from factories or other vehicles.

Bermuda's roads are narrow and winding—most of them were laid out originally for pedal bicycles (push bikes) and horse-drawn vehicles. The Tribe Roads, designed in 1616 as boundaries between the nine parishes, are much as they were in the 17th century and not more than a narrow path. Since 1946, when automobiles officially arrived on the island, the speed limit has been set at 20 mph on open roads, and 15 mph in the town of St. George and the city of Hamilton.

You can't get lost in Bermuda (at least not very) because the island is only one-and-a-half miles at its widest point and you're never too far from one of the main arteries that run east and west across Bermuda. These are the North Shore Road, South Shore Road and Middle Road, while a number of smaller roads run alongside as well as criss-cross at regular intervals. Every convenience is available for visitors who plan to cycle about. There are plenty of filling stations (even though one can do the entire island and back on a single tank of gas), and complimentary maps are available at every Visitor's Bureau, hotel desk and cycle livery. If you prefer to save your energy one way, the local ferries will carry your cycle (provided there is room) for about $1 and help you carry it on and off.

Indeed, a perfect day's excursion is to take the ferry across the Great Sound to Somerset Bridge and cycle about from there. Somerset Bridge, which links the village to the main island of Bermuda, is considered the world's smallest drawbridge. It has an 18-inch draw that opens to allow the masts of sailboats through. In addition to exploring the village of Somerset, one can have a swim on Long Bay on the northwest coast or catch a glass-bottom boat trip from Mangrove Bay over to the reefs, with a stop for snorkeling and swimming along the way. Following lunch in one of the funny local inns, take a drive out to Land's End, Ireland Island for a visit to the Maritime Museum and Royal Keepyard. On the way back to Somerset Bridge for the return ferry, don't forget to stop and rest on the grassy slopes of Fort Scaur, which offers a wonderful view of the Great Sound. Chat with the caretaker and sign the guest book (he will appreciate it).

At least one day should be spent on St. George's Island, which has more attractions per square foot than any other site in Bermuda. Wandering through the crooked streets and alleys with their funny names (Featherbed Alley, Petticoat Lane, Barber's Alley, Old Maid's Lane), one has the chance to explore 370 years of history that intertwines Bermuda, the United Kingdom and North America. Two of the island's five forts and one of its two lighthouses are in the St. George area, as well as superb beaches, and 18th-century buildings that are homes, quaint shops and inns.

Returning to the main island, one can stop off at a perfume factory, two limestone caverns that are open to the public, a bird sanctuary, and Devil's Hole where fish, turtles and sharks swim side by side. Riding along the South Shore Road offers a view of some of the most beautiful beaches in the world plus a six-mile stretch of reef known as The Boilers because of the constantly breaking surf along its top. High above is the Gibbs Hill Lighthouse and from its 245-foot elevation visitors have a spectacular sight of the Great Sound and the small islands it encompasses.

Cycling in the city of Hamilton is no problem either because there is plenty of parking available along the harbor under the same trees that provide shelter for the few remaining horse-and-carriage operators. In fact, let your cycle rest a bit and take a carriage ride around the town. Bermuda has certainly embraced the modern world but her style and dignity have not changed!

Of course, there are other ways to explore Bermuda but one has to rely on either taxis or public transportation because there are no cars for rent. Taxis are expensive (as they are anywhere in the world) but here they are great fun, especially if you pick one with a blue flag on the hood (or bonnet as Bermudians say). There are some 562 taxis on the island, of which 400 have the blue flag which means that the driver is a qualified tour guide. He or she has taken a stiff written examination as well as a practical test on courtesy and driving ability. It does not cost any more to take a "blue flag" taxi so if you feel like chatting a bit, asking a few questions on what you've seen around the island, be sure to catch one. All taxis can be hired by the hour or the day for sightseeing, and the drivers will help you plan an interesting (and convenient) itinerary.

Local buses are another easy way to sightsee and the routes of the most popular spots and what route number to look for are available (see *Getting Around* section). Bus stops are well marked along the main roads and passengers must have the correct change (60¢ for the first 3 zones, $1 for a longer ride). The courteous bus driver will tell you how much to put into the till and let you know when he has reached the destination. Buses are a friendly way to explore and you will meet some interesting people en route, both locals and visitors!

But no one should leave Bermuda without exploring, at least once, by ferry. The ferries that leave every few minutes from Hamilton for Paget, Warwick and Somerset are a wonderful experience. This is an island resort that should be seen by water, and short of having one's own private yacht, the ferry is a good substitute. It is also one of the few bargains left—$1 one way to Paget or Warwick and $2 one way to Somerset.

Guests in Paget or Warwick hotels can easily take the ferry to Hamilton for a day's shopping and sightseeing. Lovely Newstead is a short walk from the Hodsdon's Landing (10-minute ride to Hamilton); Glencoe is a five-minute walk from Salt Kettle; the Inverurie Hotel is next to Darrell's Wharf; and the Belmont Hotel is a stiff climb up the hill from the Belmont dock. The ferries run frequently from 7:15 A.M. to 11:20 P.M. during the week, and from 10 A.M. to 9:30 P.M. on Sundays and holidays.

The Somerset ferry is more exclusive and runs only from 7:05 A.M. to 5:25 P.M. from Hamilton during the week, and from 9:30 A.M. to 3:30 P.M. on Sundays. The two big stops on Somerset Island are Somerset Bridge and Watford Bridge. If you are taking a cycle along, get off at the former and catch the ferry from the latter point at the end of the day. (It's all the same price.)

These ferries are romantic because the water is a vivid blue and the scenery so lively, with pastel houses climbing up and down the hillsides. They are also a reminder of how the early settlers traveled around the island, although not in such luxury. It's doubtful that they had a closed compartment in which to take refuge from wind and rain!

SANDYS PARISH

The charming village of Somerset is the focal point of Sandys Parish, which encompasses the islands of Somerset, Boaz, and Ireland north and south. The parish is named after Sir Edwin Sandys, another of the large shareholders in the original Bermuda Company, but Somerset honors Sir George Somers, the valiant admiral of the *Sea Venture*. This whole area at the western end of the Bermuda chain is a favorite with visitors who enjoy its gentle charm, quiet lanes and sheltered coves. The area boasts two fine harbors, a handsome parish church, a fort built at the Duke of Wellington's suggestion, two nature reserves, a maritime museum, and the smallest drawbridge in the world.

Sandys begins at the end of the main island, just after the Port Royal Golf Course and near the U.S. Naval Air Station Annex. It is bisected by Middle Road, which ends at Somerset Bridge. This tiny bridge links the main island with Somerset and has a draw of 18 inches, just enough to let the mast of a small sailing vessel through. This smallest drawbridge in the world crosses an inlet between Ely's Harbour and the Great Sound, and from here one can pick up an oleander-lined byway that follows the old railroad tracks into the village of Somerset. (The narrow-gauge railroad that ran between Somerset and St. George's was taken up when automobiles arrived and shipped from Bermuda to Guyana in 1948.)

Ely's Harbour, now full of small pleasure craft bobbing on their buoys, was important to the early traders of Bermuda since it provided a quick shelter from sudden storms at sea. It was also a smuggler's haven. Overlooking it on the western shore of Sandys is Wreck Hill, the site of early fortifications. The Scaur Lodge property is an excellent spot that overlooks the harbor and Scaur Bay where cathedral rocks form interesting shapes. Overlooking the Great Sound is Fort Scaur, another of the fortifications built under the military defense scheme of the Duke of Wellington. Built into the hilltop, its series of bunkers and tunnels are surrounded by dry moats and the whole grassy area has been equipped with picnic tables. The fort's caretaker welcomes visitors and enjoys treating them to a personal tour, all the time imparting local history. Sandys' citizens have always had their own strong minds and rarely agreed with the rest of the colony on which side they should take during outside conflicts. During the American Civil War, for example, this area heavily supported the North and its Union army.

More local history can be found in the parish church of St. James, one of the loveliest churches on the island. No one knows for certain when the original church on this site was built, but it was probably of wood and destroyed by a hurricane. Part of the present structure was built in 1789, with the north and south aisles added in 1836. A century later, the church was struck by lightning and the spire fell perpendicularly into the center aisle. The present spire, designed by a local architect, is floodlit at night to show off its perfectly proportioned beauty. In addition to the polished cedar doors and interior of the church, one is impressed by the bright and happy feeling within the structure. The long driveway from the main road is lined with whitewashed graves, all glistening in the brilliant sunshine.

On both sides of Somerset Island are lovely bays and beaches for exploring and swimming. Traveling along the West Side Road, we pass Church Bay (with St. James on the hill above), Margaret's Bay and down to Daniel's Head where there is a station for the Canadian Armed Forces. In this area overlooking Long Bay is also Skeeter's Corner where an interesting murder took place last century. It seems that a local man named Skeeters killed his wife one evening because she talked too much. He tied her body to a boulder and dropped her in the bay. But the neighbors were suspicious, recovered the body, and Mr. Skeeters was convicted and executed. But this hairy tale should not detract from one's enjoyment of Long Bay which has some beautiful beaches and is an idyllic spot on this island.

Around the corner is Mangrove Bay, a bustling little area with Cambridge Beaches, the colony's oldest cottage colony at one end. From Mangrove Bay wharf, one can take sightseeing boats out to the reefs for snorkeling and swimming, or make arrangements for fishing and sailing adventures. The bay got its name from the Mangrove trees that used to line the shore but, alas, do no more.

Within the village of Somerset, there are charming shops and inns as well as quiet lanes down which to cycle or wander. It is a pleasant town that always seems just about to take a siesta (or is waking up from one). If you prefer to travel by ferry, the Watford Bridge dock is just down the road and within easy walking distance of such local spots as the Loyalty Inn, The Old Market, Somerset Historical Dioramas, Sandys Souvenir Shop, and Ye Village Corner. A ten-minute walk along Somerset Road brings us to one of the properties belonging to the Bermuda National Trust, Springfield and the Gilbert Nature Reserve.

Springfield is an old plantation home in possession of the Gilbert family from 1700 to 1973 when it was acquired by the Trust in conjunction with the Audubon Society. The property encompasses five acres of unspoiled woodland, open space and planting land that adjoins an old plantation home. Known as Springfield, the building with courtyard and separate kitchen, buttery and slave quarters is interesting as an early 18th-century Bermudian structure. The finest rooms in the house are used as the Somerset branch of the Bermuda Library and unfortunately are only open on Mondays, Wednesdays and Saturdays but the grounds are open daily.

Returning to the center of town will take you to Sugar Cane Point and Watford Bridge and on to Watford, Boaz and Ireland islands. This area extends all the way to Land's End and the Royal dockyard. Shipbuilding was the major source of income for this area and much of the work was done by convicts brought out from England and kept in close quarters on board old frigates. Sandys' people were proud of their dockyard but were often worried what would happen to the economy if shipbuilding ceased to be a major world enterprise. In the early years of this century, they found out that tourism would be the economic replacement (as Cambridge Beaches opened its doors to visitors).

The area utilized on Ireland Island North was the only fully planned dockyard in the British Empire and under control of the Royal Navy from 1837. Royal naval forces were much in evidence around the colony since the War of 1812, when campaigns such as the burning of Washington in 1814 were operated from Bermuda. A fortress was constructed by convicts around the dockyard and a Commissioner's House was built on a hill overlooking the entire area. The plan was devised as early as 1820 and guns were placed around the entire embankment. But the munitions were never needed and by the 1920s, the defences were abandoned. This inner fortification is known as the "Keepyard" and is now of interest to visitors to the Maritime Museum.

This is a splendid place, an outdoor-indoor museum that gives credence to Bermuda's three centuries of seafaring history. This museum epitomizes the hardy spirit that kept the early colonists striving onward to keep their tiny island protected while also using the sea as a constant source of commerce. It is a museum that complements visiting the fine old homesteads where sailors could relax among the local crafting of the same cedar that built their beautiful ships. One enters the museum area through an outer gate

that was originally fronted by a moat and drawbridge and in the
center of the Keepyard is a giant figure of Neptune, taken from a
ship that saw her end at the finish of the 19th century. This figure-
head was first placed near Admiralty House at Spanish Point until it
found a more living role in the new museum.

The main building, called the Queen's Exhibition Hall, was constructed by convicts of local stone in 1850 and has been beautifully
restored and lit to show off a fine display of maritime maps, models
and interesting objects pertaining to the sea. It is the type of museum that one can wander in at leisure among historic buildings used
to store munitions but now put to better use. Of especial delight is
the Bermuda Fitted Dinghy exhibit in the eastern building, which
features the 17-foot *Spirit of Bermuda* built to sail to New York in
1935 by two local men. One can also wander among the gun enplace-
ments and magazines for spectacular views of Grassy Bay and the
Great Sound. See also the Treasure House, the History of Whaling
and Turtle Fishing exhibitions.

The museum is not yet finished since there are plans to refurbish
the Commissioner's House up on the hill, which was built between
1823 and 1830 and is considered to be the most expensive residence
ever constructed on a military base. The colonial-style building has
stabling for 11 horses on the ground floor and ornate, grandiose
moldings and plastering throughout. It is supposed to be a fine example of period architecture and a contrast to the simple and functional
design that Bermudians developed for their own homes. The Maritime Museum has been the solid effort of many Bermudians intent
upon preserving their history and sharing it with visitors.

It is possible to catch the return ferry to Hamilton from the Freeport dock, very near the museum and dockyard, if you happen to be
there precisely at 4:50 P.M. daily (except Sunday). This service is
infrequent, unfortunately, and the last ferry on weekdays leaves
Watford Bridge at 5:50 P.M. and Somerset Bridge at 6:10 P.M. for the
sunset ride back to the capital.

Alternatively, one can cycle or bus back to Somerset and pick up
the floral-laden route along East Shore Road, visiting the Gladys
Morrell Nature Reserve near Cavello Bay. This two-acre area of
open space was presented to the National Trust in 1973 by the
Sandys chapter of the Daughters of the Empire in memory of Mrs.
Morrell.

The path is lined with hibiscus from about South View Road all the way to the end of the island. Just before the bridge on the east side is Lantana, a traditional and very attractive cottage colony that is enjoyable for lunch at its La Plage restaurant down below. The cycle path continues after the bridge, all the way to George's Bay Road, just before the boundary of Southampton Parish. Shortly thereafter, one can pick up Middle Road for the return journey to Warwick, Paget and the rest of the island.

SOUTHAMPTON PARISH

Southampton Parish presents a long, lean portrait from its boundary at Riddell's Bay to Tucker's Island where the U.S. Naval Air Station Annex is now situated. Named after the third Earl of Southampton, this area which has also been called Port Royal, offers a feeling of wide open spaces as well as breathtaking views of both the north and south shores.

Southampton's south shore from Stonehole Bay to Church Bay is spectacular and the public beach along Horseshoe Bay is one of the most photographed in the world. Not far out is a six-mile stretch of reef known as The Boilers because the constantly breaking surf along its top causes a boiling-like foam. The long continuous beaches along this coastline are only broken by cozy bays with craggy rocks and hardy shrubs that complement the clear blue waters. No photograph can do this area justice for not only does the sea do its constantly changing thing, but the hues and subtleties of the sparkling sands move back and forth according to their moods. There is a complete metamorphosis from the bold and brilliant stance at high noon to the soft and delicate feeling that emerges at sunset. Here, along the south shore in Southampton parish, one can indulge in special moments of deep thought for nature is as it is and man has not tampered with it too much.

The reverie is broken slightly at the Southampton Princess, high up on the hill and spilling all the way down to the sea. Located on 60 spectacular acres, the hotel is a younger sister to the Hamilton Princess and of the chain part-owned by D. K. Ludwig, the famed American entrepreneur. One story that goes around concerning the building of the new hotel is that Mr. Ludwig thought the prices quoted on the carpets (to be made in Taiwan) were too high, so he bought the carpet company and thereafter the price of the carpets was no longer a problem!

This hotel is just like an American hotel, with its ultra-modern and luxurious accommodations, suites that have plush accoutrements and marble baths and dark, heavily air-conditioned lobby and shopping areas. The property along the south shore has become a beach and tennis club area with the Whaler Inn restaurant which is hectic during the daytime but more civilized and romantic in the evening when there is dancing on the terrace. Down on the other shore is the Waterlot Inn, which also belongs to the Southampton Princess. Recently rebuilt and a most elegant place to dine, the restaurant is on the same site where an inn has been open, more or less for the past 300 years. This has been a popular spot for Bermudians because they can come to dine just as well by boat as by road (and Bermudians are far more fond of their boats than their automobiles).

In between the two shores is an 18-hole golf course, two swimming pools, shops, restaurants, nightspots, and enough guest rooms to hold 1,500 people as well as their conventions, seminars and small group meetings.

Next to the Southampton Princess is Gibbs Hill and its famous lighthouse constructed between 1845 and 1846 and the second iron lighthouse in the world. The project had first been discussed in 1830 but nothing was done until the next decade when a survey proved that a total of 39 shipwrecks had occurred off the western end of the islands during this period, on reefs that extend as far as 16 miles off the shore.

Gibbs Hill stands 245 feet high and the lighthouse, which was constructed in England and brought over in pieces by ship, is 117 feet from base to light. The beam runs 362 feet above sea level and can be seen approximately 40 miles away by ships and 120 miles away by airplanes flying at 10,000 feet. Electricity finally replaced the original burner of four circular wicks in 1952, and light is now supplied by a 1,500-watt bulb located in the center of the lens. The lens makes a complete revolution every 50 seconds. It weighs two and three-quarter tons and contains 1,200 pounds of mercury. The machinery was formerly wound by hand every 30 minutes but this too was replaced by electrical equipment in 1964 and the entire operation is now automatic.

It is an easy climb of 185 steps to visit the top of the lighthouse and inspect the impressive mechanism that makes it work. And not only can one see the highly polished brass gears of the light, but a small walkway around the top of the structure offers stupendous views of the entire Bermuda islands chain. The west end of the colony lies below, while the Great Sound and Hamilton lie beyond and just a little farther on is the unbroken expanse of open ocean.

Continuing along the South Shore Road, we come to Sonesta Beach Hotel nestled between Sinky Bay and Boat Bay. The Sonesta is another of the large and luxurious resort hotels and was designed to take full advantage of its site along the water. On the eastern side of the hotel is a pleasant cove where small craft are moored and fishermen come early in the morning to make their plans for the day. On the western side of the hotel is a charming, sandy beach in another cove where one can swim all year and hotel guests can learn the rudiments of scuba-diving from Kevin Burke before going onward to dive for sunken treasures.

At the top of the hill, overlooking Sonesta Beach, is the Henry VIII Restaurant and Pub where good food is served in a convivial atmosphere. During the warm weather, the doors and windows are opened and one can sit out on the stone terrace, overlooking the south shore. Farther along the coastline is the Reefs Hotel and its beautiful beach, plus Christian Bay and Church Bay. At the end of the parish are West Whale Bay and Whitney Bay beaches as well as the government-owned Port Royal Golf Course, an 18-hole championship course designed by Robert Trent Jones. This course is open to the public and players give it high marks for a challenging and exciting game. A pro shop, restaurant and tennis courts are all attached, so plan to spend the day.

This end of Southampton was actually considered "overplus" land when the original survey was made by Richard Norwood in

1616. This consisted of some 200 acres which the governor, Daniel Tucker, took as his own and proceeded to build himself a nice house. Naturally, this did not sit well with the shareholders of the Bermuda Company (who actually belonged to the land) so Governor Tucker was reconciled to having only a portion of this choice spot. However, the area set a Tucker family tradition that went on for several generations and we have often mentioned a Colonel Henry Tucker and his family who lived at The Grove in Southampton Parish. (Some feel that they built a stone house on the same site that their ancestor Daniel had built a wooden mansion.)

Colonel Henry Tucker is best known by us for his role in the theft of 100 kegs of gunpowder one August night in 1775 to help the American colonists in their "disagreement" with the Mother Country. He is also the father of Henry Tucker, whose house on Water Street in St. George's belongs to the National Trust and is brimming with fine mementoes of the Tucker family and its accomplishments. Colonel Henry had six children and two of them went to America to begin other branches of this fascinating family.

The little bay just before the boundary of the parish is called George's Bay (after Colonel Henry's son) and the island on which the U.S. Naval Air Station Annex is located was previously known as Tucker's Island. The spirit of this fascinating family is not far— wander around a bit and try to catch it.

RIEN SANS DEVOIR

WARWICK PARISH

Named after the second Earl of Warwick, another major shareholder in the Bermuda Company of 1610, this parish boasts a number of hotels and restaurants, two beautiful golf courses, lovely stretches of beach, and the oldest church of Scotland outside Scotland. The parish begins just past the Inverurie Hotel on the Harbour Road and near Surfside on the South Shore Road.

The Harbour Road boundary probably falls in line with Darrell's Wharf, a busy landing for the Hamilton ferry. Just opposite the dock is a beautiful old Bermudian home, one of several dotting this area. These large and elegant structures were obviously built more than a century ago, when the road was less wide and less traveled. As one passes by, it is a delight to admire their fine features in the traditional island roof, doors and windows, and the pastel exteriors. Occasionally, you can spot a water storage tank with its whitewashed top aboveground and separate buttery, both of which indicate an age gone by (modern storage tanks are built underground and refrigerators have replaced butteries).

On the harbor side of the road are some small boat building yards and off to the west is the bird-shaped Darrell's Island. The Darrell name is another Bermudian tradition and the family is widespread throughout the colony. A menu at the Waterlot Inn farther down the road (in Southampton) commemorates Claudia Darrell who ran the place during the first part of this century. Claudia might be called the island's first "women's libber," for she apparently defied custom and took on male tasks. Many articles were written about Claudia, and her personality and energy are still very much a part of the island. Darrell's Island is also remembered because it's the site of Bermuda's first airport. The seaplanes that brought visitors from New York in the early 1930s landed here.

But, returning to our slow progression down the Harbour Road, we come to the Belmont dock and above, the Belmont Hotel and Golf Club. Sitting on 110 acres, the large pink structure belongs to the Trusthouse Forte family, together with the Bermudiana Hotel in Hamilton and Harmony Hall in Paget. The Belmont is known for its lovely views overlooking the Great Sound and for its 18-hole golf course that meanders around the hill and then extends over to the far side of Middle Road. Both the golf course and the tennis courts are open to non-members (and non-guests of the hotel) for a small fee. But reservations are necessary, so pay a visit to the pro shop which is easily reached from the Harbour Road.

Continuing along Harbour Road, we turn on Burnt House Road (a name probably derivative of the 17th century when the only way to get rid of the devastating rats was to burn houses down), turning right on Middle Road and then right on Riddell's Bay Road just before the discotheque/bar called Flavors. Sitting beside a corner of the bay is the White Heron Country Inn, with its two paddle tennis courts. At the very end of the road is the Riddell's Bay Golf and Country Club, an 18-hole private course where the introduction of a member or hotel is required for visitors to be able to play. Riddell's Bay was a haven for trading ships centuries ago and was originally called White Heron Bay, but the name was changed to accommodate a local family called Riddell.

For a look at the South Shore side of Warwick Parish, we take Horseshoe Road down to the South Road and travel east, coming first to Warwick Camp. These impressive blue-and-red-signed barracks were home for British troops during two world wars and now house the volunteer Bermuda Regiment. There is an artillery range on the property so do not be alarmed at the sound of shooting in the distance.

Jobson's Cove and Warwick Long Bay offer a magnificent stretch of public beaches along the south shore with glorious cliffs and rocks and sand. One can spend the whole day here and never see it fully. This area is popular for picnics and body surfing and there are some interesting horse trails set far back from the swimming area. Motorbikes must be parked above in allotted spaces and are not allowed down on the shore. The whole area is beautifully kept and impressive at all times of the day and evening, any time of the year. A public camping area is also along this stretch of the shore.

There are a number of small housekeeping units here, which are worth a visit. The Mermaid Beach Club has a fine restaurant overlooking the water and some scenes from *The Deep* were filmed at Marley Beach. Farther along, the South Shore Beach Club is owned by the Trusthouse Forte group (which provides transportation for members of its three hotels), but visitors may spend the day for a towel and locker fee. The club has changing facilities and snacks and drinks are available.

Equestrians will want to visit the Warwick Riding School and Tack Shop which offers guided tours of Bermuda by horseback. Private or group lessons can be arranged for novices and the more advanced can take a breakfast ride along trails overlooking the pink South Shore beaches, followed by a large English breakfast served in an old Bermuda house. Bermudians are horsey people, in the tradition of their English forebears and the Bermuda Hunt Club is small but active. The tack shop at the Warwick Riding School sells caps and other paraphernalia at well below U.S. prices.

Other roads to be explored in Warwick are Spice Hill Road, Tamarind Vale, Cedar Hill and St. Mary's Road, Cobbs Hill Road and Keith Hall Road and the many Tribe Roads that cut the parish from north to south. Wandering along these byways on your motorbike, drinking in the morning glory and oleander that line the edges, while enjoying the traditional large and small houses that have been homes to generations of islanders is what Bermuda is all about.

PAGET PARISH

Paget is a parish one cannot miss. It begins at the edge of Hamilton Harbour (or end of the lake as it was commonly called), and winds around Berry Hill Road on the east, faces the city of Hamilton on the north while the south shore has some of the most beautiful and popular beaches along the colony's coastline. Named after the fourth Lord Paget, the parish has a high concentration of residences because of its proximity to Hamilton, and many of its historic homes can be viewed, at least from the outside, by visitors. There are no golf courses in the parish and few open spaces other than the 36-acre Botanical Gardens estate and Paget Marsh.

Leaving Hamilton via Crow Lane, one can reach the Botanical Gardens via Berry Hill Road, Point Finger Road or the South Shore Road. The Botanical Gardens are one of the colony's prime attractions and have steadily increased in size since 1898 when the Department of Agriculture took over the property. The gardens are still maintained by the Bermuda government and are open daily from sunrise to sunset. Conducted tours are offered on Tuesdays, Wednesdays and Fridays from 10:30 A.M. and last approximately 90 minutes.

Throughout the year, the gardens are the site of various exhibitions and shows. These include an agricultural exhibition in April; dog shows in February, May and November; poultry, citrus and bird shows; and periodic horse shows. Of the many permanent attractions, there is a garden for the blind, hibiscus garden, palm garden, cacti and succulent garden, orchid garden, aviary, and other exotic plant houses. In the center of the property is Camden House, a former private residence from one of the finest estates in Bermuda. The land, which once contained an arrowroot factory, now belongs to the gardens and the house is the official residence of Bermuda's premier. It is open to the public on Tuesday and Wednesday afternoons from 12 noon to 2 P.M. Nearby is Il Chianti, an Italian restaurant where lunch and dinner are available (as well as alcoholic beverages). Local buses stop at the west and south gates and cycles can be parked on the grounds, near where the guided tours begin.

Driving west on Middle Road, we detour down to Hungry Bay which is a popular spot for both fishermen and naturalists and where one can almost hear the sea roar like a hungry animal before an approaching storm. Nearby is Grape Bay with its lovely beach, small hotel and housekeeping cottages. Returning to Middle Road, we come to Rural Hill where there are some fine private residences including Chelston, the official residence of the U.S. Consul General. This home, which is often on the spring Garden Club tour, sits high up on 14 acres of beautiful countryside. The house was acquired from the estate of an American businessman in 1954 and is perfect for entertaining. The property extends down to the south shore and the sea is accessible by walking through an old moon gate.

Another attractive home in the Rural Hill area is Inwood, just across Middle Road, set back a bit on the north side. Part of the house was built in 1650 but additions were made in 1700 by Colonel Francis Jones who was a member of King William III's council in Bermuda. These 18th-century additions made the structure in the form of a cross, which was typical of the era. Inwood is also fea-

City Hall in Hamilton, with its tower windclock and Sea Venture weathervane, houses a small theater as well as the Bermuda Society of Arts.

Hamilton, the capital of Bermuda since 1815, is full of fascinating buildings. Above, Perot Post Office, on Queen Street, is where the island's first postage stamp was born. Below, Sessions House is the seat of Bermuda government. Visitors are welcome to view the workings of the Supreme Court (lower floor) and the House of Assembly (second floor).

Bermudians have created a harmonious style of building throughout the island. Above, the omnipresent Moongate, an idea imported from China, shows Hamilton Harbor from the steps of the Belmont Hotel. Below, Inwood is a fine example of an 18-century private home and has been in the same family for eight generations.

A popular spot to wander is St. Peter's churchyard in the town of St. George. The tombstone of American Consul John W. Howden, buried in 1852, says "We Shall Meet Again."

tured on the Garden Tour and is noted for its 12 powder rooms (where ladies and gentlemen of the day used to powder their wigs before joining the social gathering). The old cedar-beam ceilings are also an eye-catching feature.

To sidetrack a bit at this point, take the Stowe Hill Road to Rosecote, the home and studio of Alfred Birdsey, unofficial artist laureate of Bermuda. Here one can chat with the artist's son-in-law while rummaging about the small studio to look at the delightful watercolors, reproductions, and perhaps a commissioned oil painting. Birdsey has a charming style that at once captures the color and spirit of the island. He can whip up a watercolor in no time (about ten minutes) if you have a special preference and does both large and small paintings. (He has done beautiful murals in both the New York and Boston offices of the department of tourism.) Although it may not be possible to visit with Birdsey personally as he no longer gives interviews freely, one can enjoy the personality of the artist just by a visit to his studio and shop. He is as colorful as his creations (and definitely enjoys the eccentricity of age).

Continuing along Middle Road once again, one comes to Paget Marsh, a 26-acre area considered to be a gem among nature reserves. Owned by both the National Trust and the Audubon Society, the marsh contains some of the finest palmetto and cedar trees on the island as well as a mangrove swamp. This is the last place on the island where a forest remains as intact as it did when the colonists first arrived. And, because this is the only safe refuge for some of the colony's endangered trees and plants, access is limited and visitors are requested to call the Trust office (2-6483) for permission to visit the area.

Nearby the marsh is St. Paul's, the parish church, which dates from 1796 and is considered young by Bermudian standards. At this juncture, one can pick up the South Shore Road for visits to Elbow Beach, Coral Beach, and Horizons Cottage Colony. This is one of the poshest parts of the south shore and Elbow Beach is the longest and most popular strand. The Elbow Beach Hotel began as a small guest house in 1908, then called the South Shore Hotel. Subsequently many additions have been made and it is now among the largest of the resort hotels. Although the beach area is private, visitors are welcome for the day for a fee. During College Weeks, many of the springtime activities take place here.

The middle portion of the beach is public and the western end belongs to the Coral Beach Club which used to be nothing more than a pleasant little restaurant and bathing facility but has become a fine tennis club. It is a private facility and the introduction of a member is required to play. However, guests at the pleasant Horizons Cottage Colony may have the use of this beautiful beach.

The harbor-side of Paget is equally beautiful and interesting. Leaving the city of Hamilton, one takes Crow Lane around to Waterville, the headquarters of the National Trust. Dating from the early part of the 18th century, the house originally belonged to the merchant-family of Trimmingham who ran their business from here. The house is now occupied by the Bermuda National Trust in the back, surrounded by a family of tame ducks, and caretakers live in the front. On Harbour Road facing Pomander Walk is Red Hole, which was once a shipbuilding and repair center; now small craft are anchored here.

Continuing along the Harbour Road which is lined with morning glory, we pass by Clermont just before the Lower Ferry Landing. Clermont is a classic example of Bermuda Georgian architecture. It was built in 1800 by Thomas Butterfield who was then chief justice of Bermuda. The house is well-known because another chief justice, Sir Brownlow Gray, built the island's first tennis court here in 1873 and the entire Gray family were early tennis enthusiasts. From this court, tennis was introduced to the United States via Mary Outerbridge who took her equipment and a book of rules to the Staten Island Cricket Club. That was in 1874—and what has happened since!

The Hamilton ferry plies along this area in its quiet but efficient way. At the Hodsdon's Ferry Landing is the lovely guest house Newstead with its fine view of the capital. The Salt Kettle dock is just a short walk to Glencoe, Greenbank, Seaward and Salt Kettle. Glencoe, the largest of the guest facilities, was a residence when President Woodrow Wilson made many visits here and stayed in what is now Room No. 7. Glencoe looks out on its own private harbor where sunfish and dinghies are anchored and ready to set sail on the weekends.

Farther down Harbour Road is Inverurie, a hotel that began its career in 1910 and has grown sideways and upwards since. The hotel is located just before the boundary to Warwick Parish and the Darrell's Wharf landing.

Taking Cobb's Hill Road straight across the island, you run into Middle Road and the Four Ways Inn, one of the colony's best and most prestigious restaurants. Here one can dine in an old-world atmosphere, in a former Georgian-style home that was built of coral and Bermuda cedar around 1727. When the weather is friendly, the delightful courtyard becomes another dining room for both French cuisine and Bermudian specialties.

The Inn is open daily for brunch, lunch and dinner (Gourmet brunch on Sundays) and reservations are a must because both the food and the ambiance are popular with Bermudians as well as visitors. As you cycle by, take a good look because you may wish to return and spend a pleasant evening.

PEMBROKE PARISH

If you are sailing into Hamilton Harbour aboard a large cruise ship, grab a spot on the top deck to watch the vessel glide slowly among the many islands and busy water traffic. Settling safely alongside the Front Street dock never ceases to be a miracle in navigational expertise because this little harbor is always full of cargo ships, Hamilton ferries that ply back and forth in their quiet way, and the plethora of pleasure craft that give Bermuda its nickname "Land of Water."

The first view of the city of Hamilton from the deck of a cruise ship is always a thrill because one sees the Front Street shops, the stop and go traffic in front of the "birdcage" (does the policeman inside really help the flow or does he just add local color?), the horses and carriages clumped under the shady trees, the Gothic tower of Bermuda's cathedral up on the hill, and the Italiante pink towers of the Sessions House off to the right. The thrill evolves into a sense of adventure as you walk down the steps into the Customs shed and cross on to the street. *Voilà*—you are here!

Hamilton was founded in 1790, around what was then called Crow Lane Harbour, for the purpose of collecting Customs duties at the western end of the island. The town was named after Governor Henry Hamilton, but was a slow achiever until New Year's Day, 1815, when the seat of government was moved here from St. George's. There were two reasons for the move: One was the fine harbor, and the other was that residences had by now spread throughout the island and it was felt that the capital should be more centrally located.

Hamilton today comprises 150 acres, gives shelter to approximately one-quarter of the island's entire population, and is Bermuda's only city. It is part of Pembroke Parish, named after the third Earl of Pembroke, a major shareholder in the Bermuda Company in 1616 when the land was surveyed. While most of the government buildings are 19th century and pretty staid, the city does boast some romantic landmarks, of which the charming, whitewashed Perot Post Office on Queen Street is one.

William Bennett Perot was Hamilton's first and most famous postmaster, serving in the position from 1816 to 1862 when he retired at the age of 72. Perot's father, descended from a French Huguenot family, had built a large rambling structure on a few acres of land at the edge of what was then the center of Hamilton in 1814 and the whole family moved in. The excess acreage was developed into fine gardens and the estate was named Par-la-Ville.

Perot shared an annex of the main house with a friend who had an apothecary and, as he preferred to putter in his garden than do anything else, his friend Heyl often ran the post office. It cost a penny to send a letter from Hamilton to St. George (or Somerset) and the mail was carried by boat. But, alas, customers would come in after hours to leave mail for delivery but not leave the proper amount of pennies. This annoyed Perot terribly, so his friend Heyl suggested that he make "postage stamps" for sale in sheets and then customers could cut them apart and paste them on their letters. Perot could cancel the stamp when the letter was received in the post office. This was 1848 and the famous Perot postage stamp was born; today it is coveted by collectors all over the world. The Perot Post Office, where you buy stamps today, is the very building that Perot used and shared with his friend Heyl, the pharmacist.

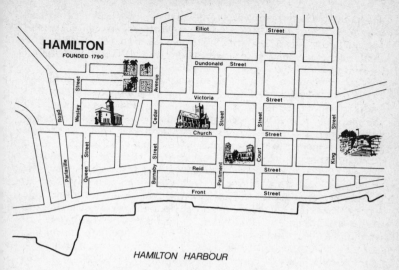

HAMILTON HARBOUR

Next door, in the comfortable family home where he brought up nine children, with its wide verandahs and enormous rubber tree (planted by Perot in 1847), is the Bermuda Library, Historical Society and Colonial Archives. The lovely gardens that Perot nurtured along and enjoyed so much are now a public park. On view in the house are a map of Bermuda believed to be drawn by Sir George Somers around 1610, his sea chest as well as portraits of him and Lady Somers painted during their lifetime. Also on view are the models of the *Sea Venture, Deliverance* and *Patience,* three ships that played an important role in the colonization of Bermuda, lovely antique cedar furniture and silver made by the early settlers, a copy of the first surveyor's map of 1616, and a sedan chair used in St. George's in the 18th century. Other objects of interest to visitors are some old coinage (hog money, it was called), a model of the famous Bermuda dinghy, and a copy of the letter that George Washington sent from his camp in Cambridge, Massachusetts, to the citizens of Bermuda in September 1775 to beg for the store of gunpowder stored on the island (before the general knew that it had already been "lifted" onto two American warships and was in possession of the Continental Congress). Mementoes of the American Civil War and the 350th anniversary celebration of the Bermuda colony are also in evidence. This is a museum well worth visiting and just small enough not to tire; take a walk in Par-la-Ville gardens afterward and think of the eccentric postmaster who created a stamp to keep his customers honest!

Walking up Queen Street and turning right on Church Street, we come upon Hamilton's City Hall on the left, a handsome modern building with a traditional Bermudian feeling and a weathervane in the shape of the *Sea Venture*. City Hall is more than just an administrative building—it is the center of the island's cultural activities. It has a fine theater where musical and dramatic performances are held, films are shown on such occasions as Olympic Day, and the upstairs hall is utilized for exhibitions and trade shows and the display of local crafts during Rendezvous Time. The building also houses an art gallery that has a revolving exhibit of local and foreign works. The cedar balustrade and large doors to the public rooms are well worth a visit. The building was designed by a local architect and contains a Time Capsule to be opened on the 500th anniversary of the colony, in the year 2109.

In the next block on Church Street is Bermuda's Cathedral of the Most Holy Trinity, dedicated in 1894 and on the site of an earlier church that was destroyed by arson in 1844. (It was the building of this cathedral that stopped construction of the church in St. George's—now known as the Unfinished Cathedral.) The structure is built mainly from native limestone with marble, granite and English oak in the decorations as well as stone from Caen (Normandy) for the moldings of doorways and windows. It is a beautiful building that is cared for tenderly by its congregation. On commemorative Sundays, for example, one can find the women of the church guild creating beautiful floral arrangements throughout the cathedral and the cushions on which one kneels have all been handmade. This makes the building a very personable one and its stained-glass windows and small chapels add to a feeling of happiness, even on a dull day. The Warrior Chapel, dedicated in 1977, contains the flags of the armed forces connected with Bermuda, two throne chairs for use on royal occasions and three kneeling desks for private prayer. High up on the east wall is the Angel Window, designed and donated by a local Bermudian artist. On the wall near the lectern is a copy of an 8th-century Canterbury Cross, given by the friends of Canterbury Cathedral and set in stones from that structure. The west doors are made from wood imported from British Guyana.

Turning down Parliament Street, one sees the new post office on the right (on the site of the famous old jail) and Sessions House on the left. In this building with its pink Italian towers, the House of Assembly meets upstairs under the portraits of King George III and Queen Charlotte, while the Bermuda Supreme Court is held on the ground floor. The Speaker of the House as well as the Chief Justice and barristers all wear the traditional English wig and black robes. There are galleries in the upper floors for visitors who may want to view a bit of "colonialism." The ornate additions to the outer face of the building were added after 1818 and the clock tower commemorates Queen Victoria's Jubilee year of 1887.

In front of Sessions House is the Colonial Secretariat, recently renamed the Cabinet Building. Built around 1840 of native limestone, it is this building in which the governor convenes parliament at the end of October, each year. He delivers an address to the legislature while standing in front of a "throne," an old Bermudian cedar chair on which is carved "Governor Josiah Forster, 1642." The Cenotaph Memorial in front of the building honors the colony's war dead, and the cornerstone was laid by the Prince of Wales in 1920 (who later became Edward VIII and abdicated to marry Mrs. Simpson). Bermudians love royalty and are always excited by visits of the royal family. Queen Elizabeth paid a visit during her coronation year, and again during her Silver Jubilee. Princess Margaret arrived on an official visit in the 1960s, and Prince Charles came to celebrate the 350th anniversary of Bermuda's parliament in 1970, and read the "throne speech" in historic St. Peter's Church where the first parliament had convened in 1620.

Across Court Street is the former City Hall, a small and compact building with beautiful cedar doors that now houses the Department of Tourism. Maps, brochures and complimentary guidebooks are available here to visitors during normal working hours. At this juncture Front Street becomes East Broadway. Turning left on King Street, you can walk or ride up to Happy Valley Road and then into Fort Hamilton for a spectacular panoramic view of the city and harbor.

During the mid-19th century, Bermuda's defense were heavily built up following a plan devised by the Duke of Wellington, hero of the defeat of Napoleon at Waterloo. The Wellington plan was to transform Bermuda into the "Gibraltar of the West" and featured the building of more forts to protect the channels. Fort Hamilton was one of the 13 fortifications built during this period that were never really needed and were outdated by the time they were completed. Closed for many years because of unsanitary conditions, Hamilton's Victorian fortification has been restored and is now considered an historic monument.

We approach the main gate over a moat, now dry and filled with exotic plants that thrive in this protected and damp area. The moat can be reached from the underground galleries and is an exciting experience to walk through. On the upper level, now a grassy slope filled with park benches, the Royal Arms of Queen Victoria are emblazoned on the main armaments. Some Bermudians even feel that the fort is the embodiment of the old queen herself, frowning down upon the city of Hamilton and its harbor.

Returning to the center of town, we walk once again down Front Street past the busy piers to Albuoy's Point, named after a 17th-century doctor who fought one of the many fever epidemics on the island. Here, next to the modern Bank of Bermuda structure, is the Visitor's Service Bureau, Chamber of Commerce, local ferries, and Royal Bermuda Yacht Club. The club itself was conceived under the calabash tree in Walsingham (that Tom Moore made famous in his poetry) by a group of keen sailors in 1844. Within a year, the group had obtained permission from the throne to use the word "Royal" and received the patronage of the royal family. The members of the club have always encouraged international racing and sponsor the glamorous Newport to Bermuda race that draws together some of the world's best sailing yachts every other year for the beginning in Newport, Rhode Island and the finish line at St. David's Head, the most eastern part of Bermuda. The yachts then sail into Hamilton Harbour and anchor off the yacht club for a few days before returning to their home port. The clubhouse, on the western side of Albuoy's Point, was actually built in the 1930s.

At the beginning of Pitt's Bay Road is a large pink structure belonging to the Bermudiana Hotel, one of two large resort properties within the city limits. The Bermudiana was originally built in the 1920s by the Furness and Withy steamship company (which also built Castle Harbour Hotel and the Mid Ocean Club in Tucker's Town) for the passengers they brought down each week on various ships. The hotel was built on the site of two well-known homes, both famous for their spacious gardens. The Bermudiana has managed to retain the feeling of living in a large garden, even though it has been built twice (the original structure burned to the ground in 1958). It has held its place in the history of tourism to the colony in this century.

Farther down Pitt's Bay Road is the Hamilton Princess Hotel, named in honor of Princess Louise, daughter of Queen Victoria, who came for a visit during the winter of 1883. This hotel has undergone a great many additions since the year after it was completed and was already too small to accommodate the number of visitors who wished to stay here!

During the early part of this century, the Princess was *the* hotel and one of the social centers of the colony for both visitors and residents attending tea dances and grand balls. Later, between the World Wars, the Princess had some competition from other new hotels going up, but she held her own and at the outbreak of World War II played her most important and exciting role. Where the beautiful people had trod in fun and finery, was now the headquarters of censorship throughout the British Empire. In the basement of the elegant Princess Hotel, experts read and analyzed mail from all over the world being carried to Europe via Pan Am flights, which were instructed to land in Bermuda between New York and Lisbon.

The Princess, which used to have spacious lawns and tennis courts, now has several additions to accommodate more people and is partly owned by the commercial empire of D. K. Ludwig, the entrepreneur from North America. It is a far cry from a hotel that was named so correctly during the Victorian era after a daughter of the queen!

Around the corner from the Princess Hotel is Pitt's Bay, a nicely protected boat anchorage for small craft and the beginning of a residential section outside the city and extending all the way to the end of the peninsula of Pembroke Parish. One of these fine old private residences is Norwood, named after Richard Norwood, Bermuda's first surveyor, who acquired the property in 1657 but the house was not built until 1707 by his granddaughter. It is well known for the amusing sign at its gate: "Where tramps must not, Surely ladies and gentlemen will not trespass." The house, which is sometimes on the Homes and Gardens Tour (organized by the Garden Club) in the spring and then open to visitors, was originally built in the shape of a cross to ward off evil spirits. There is also a maze of clipped bushes in the garden, fashioned after those in Hampton Court. It is still a unique feature of the spacious gardens. The house overlooks Pitt's Bay and Saltus Island, just before the two juts of land known as Point Share and Mill Share.

At the end of the peninsula belonging to Pembroke Parish is Spanish Point, a rather desolate rocky area where a group from the *Sea Venture* believed they found evidence that the Spaniards had camped here some years before. (It was probably Captain Diego

Ramirez who wrote a description of the islands as well as a detailed map in 1603.) At the end of the point is Cobbler's Island where executed slaves were exhibited as a warning to their colleagues.

Returning to Hamilton via Cox Hill, we pass Admiralty House which is no longer used and quite forlorn looking. It was built in the early 1800s but rebuilt many times, and one admiral known for his fondness of caves had several constructed underneath the grounds. Also on the grounds are several trees planted by visiting royalty in the late 19th and early 20th century. It was during this period that being a member of the Royal Navy was a prestige position. But since the British forces were withdrawn from Bermuda in the late 1950s, there has been no need for an Admiralty House for a long time. It is only part of a glorious and glamorous past.

Grouped in an area just north of the city boundary are the Government Tennis Stadium, St. John's Church, Black Watch Well and Pass, and Government House. St. John's, the parish church of Pembroke, was built in 1625 and stands on the site of the first church in Pembroke. Originally known as Spanish Point Church, it has been enlarged many times and its historic yard is full of the tombs of men who guided the capital and the colony along. In fact, a graveyard was the scene of an unusual drama one afternoon in 1875 when two opposing ministers arrived to read a funeral speech and each tried to outdo the other by speaking louder. Later, the resident minister of St. John's brought a "trespass" suit against the other man (from another protestant sect) and won his case. The judge fined the defendant the sum of one shilling!

From St. John's Church, we climb the hill to Mount Langton and come across Black Watch Well, which gets its name because a detachment of this famous regiment dug a well at the request of the governor during the great drought of 1849. Mount Langton is also the site of Government House, the official residence of the colony's governor. The land was purchased by the colony soon after the capital moved to Hamilton in 1815, but the original two-story structure that was on the grounds has given way to a much more impressive and imposing building. The lovely grounds are full of trees and bushes planted by important people, and it was here that Governor Hugh Sharples and his aide, Captain Hugh Sayers, were assassinated in the spring of 1973 by a local dissident.

Returning down Marsh Folly Road again, we come to the government tennis stadium where visitors may enjoy all the privileges of the tennis club as well as watch some fine local matches. Nearby, on Cedar Avenue, is Victoria Park, which was built to commemorate the queen's golden jubilee in 1887. At lunchtime, the park is full of workers in the area having a quick snack while sitting on park benches and enjoying the well-kept shrubs and indulging in a bit of "people-watching."

Hamilton has the greatest concentration of restaurants on the island and one can get simple snacks from a pushcart near the park or local specialties of freshly caught seafood from the eating places along the harbor. Most visitors prefer to sit above Front Street on the terraces of the many restaurants that line the shopping center and have their refreshments and meals while watching the people pass by below. With the colorful backdrop of small craft in the water beyond, it is a delightful scene, especially on a sunny day.

It is best to plan one's day around shopping, sightseeing, and viewing the legislature (when in session). During the winter season or Rendezvous Time (December to mid-March), the Department of Tourism plans special events for visitors such as exhibitions of local crafts in Pier One (Tuesdays) as well as noon performances of the skirling ceremony at Fort Hamilton (Wednesdays). From April to October (except August), the 16th-century ceremony of Beating Retreat can be viewed on Front Street as well as in Somerset and St. George, performed by the volunteer corps of the Bermuda Regiment and Bermuda Cadet Pipe Band. This cermony is traditionally performed at sunset, much as it was when the ancient towns of England were surrounded by fortifications and all were warned to return to the protection within before nightfall.

If you plan to spend the evening in Hamilton, most restaurants require advance reservations and the majority prefer a jacket and tie for gentlemen (see *Wining and Dining* section). The action in local nightclubs begins around 9:30 or 10 P.M. and winds down in the wee hours of the morning. Taxis can always be found in the area but have a surcharge after midnight so be sure to carry enough cash!

DEVONSHIRE PARISH

Wandering through Devonshire Parish is a bit like wandering around the back roads of the English countryside. For this area of Bermuda seems to be more lush, more green and more hilly than the rest of the island. There are few commercial enterprises here that appeal to visitors, just a few housekeeping apartments and one cottage colony (along the south coast), no restaurants and just one very large nightspot, the Clay House Inn, along the north coast. Named

after the first Earl of Devonshire, the parish does boast a public golf course, marsh land, a nature reserve, some gardens, and an historic old church.

Old Devonshire Church stands smack in the middle of the parish on the Middle Road. Built plain and simple like an early Bermuda cottage, the foundation of this building was erected around 1716 although the first structure on this site dates from 1624. It is known as Old Devonshire Church although it was formerly called Christ Church. Unfortunately what we visit today is a reconstruction since 1970 when the old building was largely demolished by an explosive placed in it on Easter Sunday of that year. Many beautiful and historic pieces were lost in the fire that resulted, including the font and organ, but others were saved and restored.

The building is constructed of local limestone and cedar, following the early shipwright technique. The vestry is to the north, the chancel to the east. An extension in 1806 is still evident in the west wing and built to house the organ loft. All of the pews face the three-tiered pulpit and communion table which are both believed to be from the original 17th-century church, and fortunately were saved in the 1970 fire. Some pieces of church silver dates from 1590 and are said to be the oldest pieces on the island. A cedar chest, believed once to have held the church records, also dates from the early 17th century for it was obviously built before the Bermuda Company forbade the use of timber cedar for the making of chests around 1650. Other pieces that have survived are an old cedar armchair, candelabra, cross and cedar screen. Until the fire, there was no electricity in the church and evening services were by candlelight, but small fans now appear in the plain-glass windows so we can assume that the structure is properly wired. The building has a cool, puritan feeling and is a soothing place to visit on a warm day.

Nearby is Devonshire Marsh, or what the Bermudians refer to as a "brackish pond." In the early days, Devonshire was called Brackish Pond; today there is a large distillation plant in the parish as well as subterranean wells that supply a great deal of fresh water to the island. So this early name was apt as the parish is full of water, brackish or not.

The north coast of Devonshire is craggy and full of cliffs. Again one might think of England except for the beautiful turquoise sea that places Bermuda apart from almost anywhere else in the world. Close to the border of Pembroke is Devonshire Dock where local fishermen come in the afternoon to measure their catch. This is a good place to buy dinner if you are staying in a housekeeping unit. If not, it's just a good place to pick up some salty jargon.

Along the south coast of Devonshire is the lovely cottage colony called Ariel Sands with its own private beach as well as Devonshire Bay with its public beach area. Halfway between the two are geologic exposures that show three stages of development in the formation of the islands.

Along the South Shore Road are two other places of interest. The Edmund Gibbons Nature Reserve (just west of the junction with Collector's Hill) is marshland that provides living space for a number of birds and rare species of Bermuda flora. It is open daily and visitors are advised not to enter the marshy area. Just west of Devonshire Bay Road is the Palm Grove Garden, set behind a beautiful old traditional home that faces the South Road. It is open daily (except Sunday) from 9 A.M. to 5 P.M. The private estate also has a fine collection of tropical birds.

The arboretum, along Corkscrew Hill Road, is another natural area that is worth a visit on a hot day. Take a stroll among the cool trees, especially fragrant after a brief rain.

Devonshire's public 9-hole golf course is called the Ocean View Golf and Country Club and is open to visitors for a green's fee. Stop by and pay a visit to the pro, Eardley Jones, and make arrangements for a lesson or a game.

Other interesting areas to visit in Devonshire are Fort Hill and Montpelier Road, Orange Valley Road and Parsons Road, Jubilee, Brighton Hill and Hermitage roads. The names alone are enough to entice anyone to take a little ride on the motorbike.

SMITH'S PARISH

Bordering Harrington Sound on the east and the open sea on the north and south, Smith's Parish was named after Sir Thomas Smith, another prominent benefactor of the Bermuda Company. The parish encompasses Flatts Village, two lovely bird sanctuaries, a superbly restored 17th-century home, and Spanish Rock, which may or may not give a clue about early visitors to the island. Local historians cannot agree on the significance of this rock on which crude carvings were found.

During the 17th and 18th centuries, Flatts was a smuggler's haven and ships used to stop here in the dark of night to unload their goods before continuing on to the eagle eye of the Customs officials at St. George's. Today this little village with old-world charm and lovely views of both the inlet and Harrington Sound is just a shadow of its former self, with a few small shops, cycle liveries, a marine center and the rambling, pink Coral Island Hotel. The hotel, which began life as a residence and then became a boardinghouse, now has the atmosphere of a country inn, with new management and both deluxe and time-share accommodations. Nearby is the Palmetto Bay Hotel.

Taking Harrington Sound Road out of Flatts Village, there are breathtaking views of the sound along an oleander-lined byway. Just past the juncture of Knapton Hill Road, you come to Devil's Hole. which might be called Bermuda's first visitor attraction. Originally a fish pond, the owner (a Mr. Trott) decided to build a wall around it in 1830 and within a few years, he was charging an entrance fee. All types of fish and turtles swim peacefully together here in what was probably a cave. For a fee, you can tug on the baited but hookless line and have some fun. You can tell big fish stories back home because whatever you catch must go back.

Also in the Devil's Hole vicinity is the former National Trust property known as Winterhaven Farm Cottage. Now owned by a local real estate firm, the cottage is no longer open to the public. Continuing on Harrington Sound Road, we come to the North Nature Reserve at the western end of Mangrove Lake and just inside the boundary of Smith's Parish. The reserve features living mangroves that attract several unique types of birds as well as other water flora and fauna. The reserve is open daily and there is no admission fee.

Returning along the South Shore Road, we pass by Pink Beach Club and cottages, a deluxe cottage colony with its own private beach and John Smith's Bay, and Spanish Rock. Located between Spittal Pond, the most spectacular of the nature reserves, and the shore, Spanish Rock has long been a riddle to the colonists. A cryptic inscription was found by the early settlers, crudely carved on a high bluff overlooking the ocean. The original inscription had a "TF" and the date 1543 and was believed to be attributed to a Spanish explorer of the 16th century named Theodore Fernando Camelo. Others feel that Portuguese explorers may have been in the area during this period and left their mark. Local historians do not agree and it makes for a lively argument. However, like Plymouth Rock, the original Spanish Rock is no longer and what one sees is but a bronze cast.

The adjoining 60-acre Spittal Pond is a wildlife sanctuary preserved by both the National Trust and the Bermuda Audubon Society, and a nature lover's paradise for long walks and observation. Between November and May, about 25 species of waterfowl come to roost. Spittal Pond is open daily and visitors are advised to please keep to the pathways provided.

Continuing on the South Shore Road, we turn right at Collector's Hill for Verdmont, a fine example of a 17th-century Bermuda mansion and the most important of the Trust properties. Now open as a museum, the structure of the house is practically unchanged since it was built sometime between 1616 and 1662 and is a lesson in exactly how these early buildings were designed. (Although the house was lived in continuously until the 1950s, it never had inside plumbing or electricity.)

Verdmont was most likely built by Captain William Sayle, who owned 50 acres of property that stretched from the north shore to the south shore and chose this hill as the site of his home. Sayle was three times governor of Bermuda; in between, his free-loving spirit led expeditions to colonize the island of Eleuthera in the Bahamas as well as a part of South Carolina. He was as colorful a character as he was a staunch Cromwellian and died in 1671 while serving as the first governor of South Carolina.

The house eventually landed in the hands of Thomas Smith, a Customs collector, who sold his house in St. George's to Henry Tucker (now the President Henry Tucker House) in 1775 when he moved to Verdmont. One of his daughters married John Green, who also became a Customs collector as well as a highly regarded portrait artist. Some of Green's portraits, including a miniature self-portrait, are now hanging in the house. The home was subsequently inherited by minor relations (the Greens had no children) and the last person to live in Verdmont was an eccentric spinster who lived there for 75 years and refused to make any modern improvements such as installing electricity or plumbing. When she died in 1953, Verdmont was purchased by the Bermuda Historical Monuments Trust (predecessor to the National Trust), renovated, and opened as a museum.

Entry to the house is now by the back door or north side of the building, next to what is considered the handsomest early stairwell in Bermuda. The newel posts on each landing were designed with removable caps so that candles could be placed at strategic intervals in the evening. Early staircases were, of course, made by hand of local cedar and one has the impression here that they became much-admired showpieces (and that much time must have been spent polishing them each day).

The house is large and square, with double chimneys on either side to provide a fireplace in every room. This was strictly for comfort as cooking and other necessities were handled outside in an attached building. Each room also has three large windows with splendid views of both shores, and some still have the old, iridescent glass. The window shutters are on the inside, in Williamsburg fashion, and not in the typical island tradition of "push out" blinds that were copied from the Caribbean. The absence of shutters or blinds on the outside does give the building a rather naked look and causes one to wonder how the old glass could have withstood storms all these centuries.

The house is furnished in English and Bermudian antiques, most of which have been lent by local residents. The downstairs rooms include a library, parlor, drawing room and dining room. Upstairs are four identical rooms now furnished as a bedroom, nursery, upstairs parlor, and Oriental room. One cannot be quite sure that the avid interest much of the Western world had in the Orient in the 18th century was shared by the colonists, but nevertheless, enough antiques of the period were found on the island to warrant such a room. In what is now furnished as an upstairs parlor (but was undoubtedly a proper bedroom) is a china coffee service reputed to be a gift from Napoleon to George Washington. But the American statesman never received his gift because the ship bringing it across the Atlantic was seized and brought to Bermuda. Its cargo was condemned as contraband under the order of John Green (who owned Verdmont). It was sold at auction and the coffee service was purchased by a Bermudian whose descendants eventually donated it to the Verdmont museum. (Is that why John Green is smiling in his miniature self-portrait?)

There is a lovely little balcony on the second floor from which to view the south shore. But it is the attic that is shrouded in mystery and many questions remain unanswered. Not only does the open-well staircase continue on to the attic, but the attic itself covers almost the entire floor plan and has a headroom of over seven feet. Some feel that the top floor staircase was added a century after the house was built and that the attic was also developed. But one wonders why—was there an overload on the family quarters or was there some secret privateering happening? Verdmont has many secrets.

Without a doubt this is one of the island's most intriguing spots to visit.

HAMILTON PARISH

This parish offers a number of sightseeing attractions as well as a diversity in scenery and natural phenomena. Named after the second Marquis of Hamilton, the parish winds around three-quarters of Harrington Sound which is actually a saltwater lake some six miles long. The parish also borders the Atlantic Ocean on the north and south and Castle Harbour on the east. The southern section of the parish, tucked between Smith's and St. George's, houses half of the

Mid Ocean golf course as well as two other brackish ponds, Mangrove Lake and Trotts Pond, which boast a full complement of fascinating water flora and fauna.

The western boundary of Hamilton parish is Flatt's Inlet where Bermuda's aquarium has resided since 1928, with a collection of sea life that ranks high in the world. Noted as the island's top tourist attraction, the aquarium has 33 tanks ranging in size from five gallons for a sea horse family to 40 feet for the long reef tank. On display at one time are about 75 of the 300 species of marine animals that inhabit the seas around Bermuda. All the fish are caught locally and the tanks are supplied with fresh water from Harrington Sound.

The aquarium has become a zoo as well for there are tortoises from the Galapagos, an open aviary for tropical birds, flamingo, and lots of monkeys. There are also two harbor seals from Labrador. Connected to the aquarium and zoo complex is a natural history museum that houses specimens of Bermuda's game fish, rare seashells, artifacts recovered from sunken ships, and local crafts of Bermuda cedar.

Following the North Shore Road around to Bailey's Bay, we pass a long stretch known as Shelly Bay, which was a major shipbuilding area from the 17th to 19th centuries. The bay was named for one of the passengers aboard the *Sea Venture*, who discovered it while exploring this end of the island. Just before Bailey's Bay, Crawl Hill is the highest point in the parish and offers superb views of the north shore. Digress a minute and turn down Trinity Church Road to Church Bay on Harrington Sound. Here amid a peaceful setting is the Hamilton parish church, originally built with just one long room in 1623. Over 350 years of reconstruction and loving care have made this into one of the most delightful churches in the entire colony and certainly worth a detour.

Returning to the North Shore Road, we come to Bailey's Bay, also named for a 17th-century citizen, and now used to refer to the whole northeastern part of the parish. Continuing on the North Shore Road is the Lili Perfume Factory, established in 1931 and a successful enterprise ever since. Free guided tours are offered daily. The tour guide explains the process of cultivating the flowers (lily and passion flowers are the favorites), extracting the scent, preserving it, and combining it with alcohol to make the perfume. These fragrances are noted for their sweetness and are made for both men and women. They can be bought at the factory and shipped worldwide for a nominal fee. On the lovely grounds of the perfume factory is a quaint gift shop housed in what looks like a miniature English cottage.

Another interesting "factory" to visit is a short step away on Blue Hole Hill. Bermuda pottery is made and sold here in a studio/workshop atmosphere. Visitors are welcome to view the creation of locally made pottery freely. Blue Hole Hill is also the home of the Blue Grotto Dolphin Show where the famous fish perform all their tricks and acrobatics in a lovely setting. Every day is the day of the dolphins and there are five shows between 11 A.M. and 4 P.M. (Admission is about $2.50 for adults, half-price for children under 12.)

The whole area between Bailey's Bay and Castle Harbour Hotel is full of caves, most of which were only discovered in this century. They have such colorful names as Admiral's Cave, Prospero's, Cathedral, Church, Crystal and Leamington. Both Leamington and Crystal caves are open to the public and have been equipped with wooden foot bridges to walk across the clear, subterranean lakes as well as floodlights that make the stalactites and stalagmites even more translucent and dramatic.

Crystal Cave was discovered in 1907 when two young boys were playing ball and it disappeared into a hole in the ground. When they burrowed after the ball, they found themselves in a vast cavern surrounded by fantastic shapes of stalag formations. The cave they found is 120 feet below the surface, now reached by a wet, sloping walkway. A guide explains the formations and then works wonders with the lighting system to make such dramatic silhouettes as the

New York skyline and Disneyland characters. If you like to go underground, you should not miss either of these commercial enterprises.

Grotto Bay Beach and Tennis Club has two caves on its property. One is called Cathedral Cave and can only be explored on hands and knees, and with permission of the management. The other, Prospero's Cave, has been turned into a popular discotheque and is quite a lively place to see. (Some say that Shakespeare took refuge here and wrote *The Tempest,* but don't believe a word of it!)

Before we take leave of the Bailey's Bay area and its caverns, we should mention two popular dining spots. The Swizzle Inn is a favorite rest stop for cyclists and bills itself as the home of the Rum Swizzle, which might be called Bermuda's national drink. Here one can sit on the small terrace and watch the traffic while enjoying a refreshing Rum Swizzle and a Swizzleburger, another house specialty. In the evening, the inn is full of locals who stop by for a chat with friends and a good game of darts and, of course, a swizzle or two.

Next to the Leamington Cave is a small branch of Trimingham's as well as the Plantation Restaurant, which features Bermudian food in a casual atmosphere. This restaurant is one of the few places on the island that offers a table d'hote menu and is well worth a visit.

Continuing along Harrington Sound Road with its peaceful scenery, we see a sign that says "Tom Moore's Tavern" and follow the arrow down a long path to Walsingham Bay. This is the home with its calabash tree that was immortalized by the Irish poet Tom Moore during his four-month visit to the colony in 1804. The bay is another named after one of the castaways on the *Sea Venture,* and when Samuel Trott, a local magistrate, bought the property in the 17th century and built a family home, it was naturally named Walsingham.

The home remained in the Trott family for several generations. Tom Moore came here to visit a descendant (also named Samuel Trott) and his daughters, and to sit under the calabash tree in the front yard where he composed romantic verse. It is this same tree that a group of gentlemen sailors sat under in 1844 to form the Royal Bermuda Yacht Club. The house was turned into a tavern about 75 years ago, with Moore's poetry lining the walls of the back room, while the bar serves up something called a "Tom Moore Special." The woods that surround the old house are much the same as they were three centuries ago, and it is pleasant to sit on the dock overlooking Walsingham Bay. In the evening, the house and grounds are especially romantic and you may feel compelled to write your own love poetry while partaking of local seafood. Tom Moore would enjoy it now also!

Overlooking Castle Harbour, on an impressive piece of property, is one of the colony's largest and most elegant resort hotels. Commissioned by the Furness-Withy Steamship Line in 1929, the hotel opened in 1931 complete with an 18-hole golf course on its 260 acres. It is a splendid property, adjacent to the famous Mid Ocean Club which the steamship line had developed a decade earlier. During World War II, the hotel was occupied by the U.S. forces but it has been restored to its former elegance—and more—in the ensuing 35 years.

Continuing on Harrington Sound Road, one jogs slightly into Tucker's Town proper and St. George's Parish and then again into the southern extension of Hamilton Parish. The hibiscus-lined road continues all the way around the sound and back up to Flatt's Village. Alternatively, you can turn left on Paynters Road for a ride through the golf course and then along the south shore, passing Trotts Pond and Mangrove Lake. The views are splendid on both routes.

ST. GEORGE'S PARISH

St. George's Parish is often called the genesis of Bermuda because it is here at the eastern end of the islands where colonization all began. On a reef off what is now called St. Catherine's Point, the *Sea Venture* carrying 150 passengers to the Jamestown settlement was wrecked in 1609. The *Sea Venture* was one of seven vessels that sailed from Plymouth, England, in May of that year to carry provisions and colonists to the new and struggling settlement on the James River (Virginia). About a week from the coast of the New World, the *Sea Venture* encountered a severe storm and was blown off course. Land was sighted after some bad days in the rolling sea, but before the little vessel could make her way into a harbor, she was thrown upon a reef and totally wrecked. Under the careful guidance of Sir George Somers, admiral of the fleet, and Sir Thomas Gates, who later became governor of Jamestown, all 150 passengers on board landed safely and took up residence for almost a year on St. George's Island. (See *Early History* section.)

The castaways built two new ships, the *Deliverance* and the *Patience*, and sailed away in the spring of 1610 for Jamestown. But they knew they had found a beautiful spot in the Atlantic Ocean and two years later, the same company that founded Jamestown sent fifty-odd adventurous folk to settle this lovely isle. They arrived in 1612 aboard the *Plough* and (after a brief stop on Smith's Island) founded the town of St. George, named after Sir George Somers and St. George, the patron saint of England. Walking through this delightful town, which has not changed much since the 17th century, one cannot help but feel a sense of history and the footsteps of these early settlers on the well-worn paths. This remained the capital of Bermuda for 203 years, until a move to Hamilton in 1815 was precipitated by the fact that the harbor was better for trading ships and that the island's capital should be placed in the center of its inhabitants.

King's Square is the heart of St. George, with its cedar replicas of Stocks and Pillory, Town Hall, Visitors' Bureau, and bridge leading to Ordnance Island. Off the square to the west is Water Street where one can find the post office, President Henry Tucker's home and Somer's Wharf.

The cedar replicas of Stocks and Pillory are a source of fun for all ages and no one should miss the opportunity to be photographed with head or feet in them! The original models stood on this site some 300 years ago and, according to legend, were in good use. Another form of punishment in the 17th century was the Ducking Stool, which can be seen on Ordnance Island. One wonders which would be worse, dunked in the cold sea several times or spending the day in the stocks. Both, apparently, were accompanied by much jeering from the townfolk.

The beautifully restored Town Hall follows the lines of the original building that was erected in 1782 and is still in use as the administrative headquarters of the town. Inside, one can admire the highly polished cedar furnishings as well as a fascinating collection of old documents and letters. The top floor was once used for entertainment. Sign the guest registry and then pay a call at the Visitors' Bureau opposite, where the staff is always courteous and most helpful.

The *Deliverance,* a replica of one of the first ships built on the island in 1609, was commissioned by the Bermuda Junior Service League and launched as a visitor attraction in 1971. The original *Deliverance* was built on St. George's Island with native cedar as well as salvage from the wreck of the *Sea Venture,* while the smaller sister-ship *Patience* was actually built on Ordnance Island. These two vessels carried about 150 people from Bermuda to Jamestown in 1610 in very cramped quarters. Exploring the replica gives one an appreciation of just a few of the hardships the early settlers endured.

Returning to King's Square, walk past the Town Hall and turn right to the old State House, the oldest building in Bermuda and commissioned by Governor Nathaniel Butler in 1620 soon after he convened the colony's first Parliament in St. Peter's Church that same year. (Bermuda's parliament is the third oldest in the world, after Iceland and England.) The State House was the first building

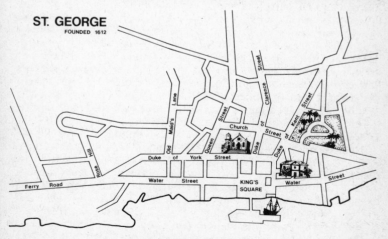

ST. GEORGE'S HARBOUR

on the island constructed entirely of native limestone and was built
in the Italianate style because Governor Butler believed Bermuda to
be on the same latitude as Italy (it is not), and the small windows and
flat roof were a deterrent against savage storms. Since 1815, when
the capital moved to Hamilton, the State House has been in trust to
the Masonic Lodge at an annual rent of one peppercorn, collected
each year in a colorful ceremony in April. However, there is serious
talk that the State House will be reclaimed by the government,
restored, and opened to the public as the historical monument that it
is.

Catty-corner from the State House is Bridge House, an 18th-
century home that now belongs to the National Trust and houses an
art gallery. It was called Bridge House because there was a small
bridge in front of the structure, to allow safe crossing of a murky
creek that has long since been filled in. According to legend, Bridge
House was the home of two governors of the colony as well as a
haven for an American violinist during the Revolution. Walking
through Reeve Court and Pound Alley (famous for a murder and
hanging 153 years ago), we come to Duke of York Street and the
entrance to Somers Gardens, a former swamp land.

To the left as you enter, a large tablet erected in 1876 commemorates Sir George Somers and his death in Bermuda in 1610. When Sir
George and his party reached Jamestown in the *Deliverance,* they
found the settlers starving so they immediately set sail for these
newly discovered islands of Bermuda to gather more provisions.
But the journey was too much for Sir George and he died soon after
his second arrival in St. George's. So, his nephew and companion,
Matthew Somers, buried his heart in the vicinity of these gardens
but took the body back to England. (No one knows for sure where
the heart is actually buried, if it is, but here is the memorial and a
lovely park named after the man who led the expedition responsible
for the eventual settling of the Bermuda colony.)

A walk through the gardens and up the hill brings us to one of the
most eloquent spots in town, the Unfinished Cathedral. This elegant
Gothic stone structure was begun in 1874 as a replacement of St.
Peter's Church, but work was abandoned after a few years because
of a schism within the church and Bermuda's only cathedral was
eventually built in Hamilton. Although abandoned, this unfinished
structure has a majestic feeling and the cacti and palm trees that
grow where the nave was intended add a certain poetry to the place.

Down the Duke of Kent Street is the Historical Society. Formerly
a home built in 1725, this museum contains antiques that show how

Bermudians lived over two centuries ago as well as an old printing shop. In front of this building in 1801, a Methodist missionary named John Stephenson preached to blacks. Since this was against the law, he was promptly fined 50 English pounds and imprisoned for six months. Undaunted, he continued to preach from his cell window, which can be seen in the basement of the present post office on the corner of Water and Queen streets. Turning right on Featherbed Alley (so named because the inebriates used to "sleep it off" here), the Print Shop houses a working model of a 17th-century press.

From Church Street, you can enter the churchyard of St. Peter's, the site of the oldest Anglican church in the western hemisphere. The yard itself is full of history and wandering among the tombstones is to replay the events of this small town. One of the most often-mentioned graves in this yard is that of Richard Sutherland Dale, an American seaman who was the last victim of the War of 1812. His parents erected the monument and inscribed it with their gratitude for the kind treatment Dale received from the citizenry of St. George's, after he was wounded and taken from his warship to a local hotel.

Other tombs worth mentioning include that of U.S. Consul John W. Howden who was buried in 1852, a victim of a yellow fever epidemic. His gravestone reads, "We Shall Meet Again." In another part of the yard is more modern history. Buried at the wish of their widows are the late governor, Sir Richard Sharples, and his aide, Captain Hugh Sayers, who were assassinated on the grounds of Government House in 1973. The assassin was executed in the fall of 1977, a deed that led to brief unrest around the island and some destruction of property by a group in the black community.

The pride of St. George is St. Peter's Church which, as noted before, is the site of the oldest continually used Protestant church in the western hemisphere. The original wooden structure on this site was erected in 1617 and the present building dates from 1713. The handsome cedar altar, placed at one side rather than opposite the front entrance, was built in 1624 and the three-tiered pulpit is considered unique. The English-ironstone font is believed to be 15th century and King William III presented the silver communion service. The walls of the church are also full of memorials to the town's historic figures, including Joseph Stockdale, the island's first printer, who died in 1803, and a much-admired governor, Alured Popple, who died in 1744 of the "fever."

Returning to Church Street and up Broad Alley (it was the widest in town), one can visit the Old Rectory on Tuesdays and Saturdays. A property of the National Trust, the rectory is a charming old Bermuda cottage built about 1705 by a reformed pirate. Its name comes from the fact that the Reverend Alexander Richardson, known as the "little bishop," lived here in the late 18th century.

Straight on is Printer's Alley named in honor of Joseph Stockdale, who came to Bermuda in 1783 with his printing press and published the *Bermuda Gazette* for 20 years. After his death, his three daughters continued the newspaper. The house in which Stockdale lived is now occupied by an editor of the *Royal Gazette,* the island's only daily newspaper. Nearby is Hillcrest, a small guest house with wide verandas and a moon gate on its spacious lawns. Among its famous guests was the Irish poet Tom Moore, who stayed here for four months in 1804 and wrote romantic verse to Hester (Nea) Tucker who lived next door. Later, the Tuckers moved up to Rose Hill where the old St. George Hotel used to stand as a prominent reminder of glorious days and the once flourishing steamboat trade.

Two interesting lanes take you down to Duke of York Street. One, Silk Alley or Petticoat Lane, got its name in 1834 when two just-emancipated slave girls walked down here with their newly acquired rustling silk petticoats. The other is called Old Maid's Lane because, well, some old maids lived along here a century ago.

Coming around to Water Street, you are in front of the town's most historic old home, the President Henry Tucker House. At the time it was built in 1752, the house was not hanging over the street but rather faced a broad expanse of lawn that went down to the harbor. The house was acquired in 1775 by Henry Tucker, eldest son of Colonel Henry Tucker of the Grove, Southampton, and the husband of the governor's daughter. During the American revolutionary years, he was president of the town council and always in a rather precarious position regarding his family's loyalties in the war between the American colonies and the Mother Country. The Tucker family was bitterly divided over this war because two of the Tucker children were living in America, one in Williamsburg, Virginia, and the other in Charleston, South Carolina. Colonel Tucker tried to remain neutral but could not and finally became the central figure in a secret campaign to help the American colonists.

By the mid-18th century, Bermuda was dependent upon the American colonies for food and faced starvation if their ships were cut off because of the revolution. Although most Bermudians were loyal to the Mother Country and had no desire to sever ties, they did not wish to go hungry. So Colonel Henry Tucker led a delegation to the Continental Congress in Philadelphia to beg that the supply of provisions to the island be continued without interruption. However, the Congress was not particularly responsive because the Bermudians could only offer salt in return for food and the Americans wanted gunpowder.

It so happened that there was a large store of gunpowder in St. George's and one mid-August night in 1775, the gunpowder found itself on two American warships that were waiting off the island in Tobacco Bay. When the governor found out about the theft the following morning, he was furious. Suspecting the Tucker family, he refused to speak to any member except his son-in-law, Henry. However, the island continued to be supplied with food throughout the war, so no questions were asked.

Portraits of Colonel Henry Tucker and his son St. George Tucker hang in the museum/house along with mementoes of the entire family that reached from Bermuda to the U.S. and England. Much of the furniture in the house was presented by a Robert Tucker of Baltimore, who died at the age of 102 in 1950. During the American Civil War, the house belonged to Aubrey Harvey Tucker, who rented his kitchen to a black slave from South Carolina named Joseph Hayne Rainey, who set himself up as a barber. (A lane outside the kitchen door has been called Barber's Alley ever since.) Rainey returned to his home state after the war and was the first black man elected to Congress. (The President Henry Tucker House is also owned by the National Trust.)

Across the street is the Carriage Museum where one can spend a delightful hour admiring the custom-built vehicles that traveled along the island's roads before the automobile arrived in 1946. The collection, begun by Mrs. Bernard Wilkinson in the late 1940's, includes everything from small children's runabouts to the most elegant and dignified carriage made. Some of them are the type one can only read about in historical novels, like the Brougham, Semi-Formal Phaeton, Vis-a-Vis Victoria, Barouche, and Opera Bus.

The Carriage Museum on Somer's Wharf is part of the multimillion-dollar restoration project that has been taking place along St. George's waterfront. Derelict warehouses, masterpieces of solid brick architecture, have been turned into a fine new eating place (The Carriage House Restaurant) and shops that are local branches of downtown Hamilton stores (The Irish Linen Shop, Trimingham's). It's a nice blending of the old with the new, and well worth a wander about the area. Keep going. Another new block of shops plus the Crown and Anchor Pub have opened.

Back along Water Street again is the post office facing onto King's Square. This is the former jail where, among other happenings, the Reverend John Stephenson was imprisoned and continued to preach to the blacks from his cell. The barred window in the basement is supposed to be the cell in which Stephenson spent six months. The pink structure on the corner of the block is the Confederate Museum and site of the old Globe Hotel. During the American Civil War (1861-5), this end of the island sided with the southern confederates, not for any moral reasons but purely business ones. The town of St. George became the focus of gun-running between the South and Europe, trading much-needed ammunition for cotton that Europe sorely wanted and were cut off from because of the northern blockade. Headquarters for these activities were on the top floor of this building (which had once been Government House when Governor Samuel Day lived here in 1700). During this period, the town's warehouses were bulging with goods and those involved in the war efforts became the "New Rich." However, this sudden wealth for St. George's, depressed from the capital's move to Hamilton in 1815, did not last long and the town soon returned to its somnolent, debt-ridden state. The Confederate Museum, also the property of the National Trust, houses an interesting collection of exhibits about this once-glamorous period.

Before collecting your motorbikes for the ride to Gates Fort and Fort St. Catherine, stop for a minute at the White Horse Tavern, where customers throw bread crumbs to the carp who are so tame by now that they expect their three meals a day. This tavern was the former home of a man named John Davenport who became very rich in the mid 1800s but had no bank in which to deposit his money, so he kept it in kegs in his basement. Upon his death, it took his sons several days to unload the cellar and count the silver and gold packed in each keg. It eventually amounted to over 75,000 English pounds, an enormous sum at that time!

Taking Water Street out of King's Square (past the old State House), you branch into Cut Road to Gates Fort, one of the oldest fortifications on the island and built between 1612 and 1615 under the direction of the colony's first governor, Richard Moore. Moore was crazy about building forts because he feared attack by the Spaniards at any time. The fort is named after Sir Thomas Gates, who was on the shipwrecked *Sea Venture* and later became governor of Jamestown. Like most of the early forts, this one was originally built of wood but replaced with stone because the site was so advantageous to defense. The small fort still flies the Stuart flag, a relic of English history when James VI of Scotland became James I of England. Around the bend are the ruins of Fort Alexandra overlooking Building's Bay, where crew members of the *Sea Venture* built the original *Deliverance* to take them to Jamestown. Riding along Barry Road by the sea is St. Catherine's Point, off which the *Sea Venture* was wrecked on the reefs, and Fort St. Catherine.

This fort on the northeastern tip of Bermuda guards the principal channel and all large ships, including luxury cruise vessels, must pass under the nose of these guns. This fort was also one of Governor Moore's projects and has been rebuilt many times, right up to this century. It is one of the island's major tourist attractions and the beaches on either side are considered close to heavenly (the Holiday Inn spills down to one of them). Not a shot was ever fired from this fort—perhaps the imposing sight of its fortifications were enough to scare away intruders. The fort is now fully restored and the underground galleries and magazines tell us what life was like in days gone by as a group of dioramas depicting scenes from the colony's history can be viewed in one darkened gallery. Upstairs, there are some replicas of the British Crown Jewels.

There is now only one golf course on St. George's Island—the 9-hole course surrounding the Holiday Inn (where you can also rent tennis courts). There are plans, however, to add this course to the former Rose Hill Golf Club course (now closed) and thus have a proper, professionally-designed 18-hole golf course in this area when the new hotel is finished on the old St. George site.

Leaving the island of St. George, one skirts over Severen Bridge and past the U.S. Naval Air Station to St. David's Head and Lighthouse Hill. This area was originally three separate islands, Longbird, St. David's and Cooper's, but were joined together through land fill in 1941 when the U.S. government was given a 99-year lease to construct a naval base that played a prominent role in World War II. Needless to say, most Bermudians did not like the fact that almost two square miles of their precious land was being pushed about and turned over to a military facility; but time has healed some of the wounds and the story of Bermuda's role during the war is a fascinating tale.

St. David's folk are, by tradition, more individual and hardy than the other islanders because they live at the most eastern and isolated point of Bermuda. Also by tradition, they have been sailors and fishermen and even the local seafood in the unpretentious restaurants out here seem to taste better than in other places on the island. Shark is a specialty and if you wish to try it, stop in at the Black

Horse Tavern or Dennis's Hideaway for shark hash or turtle steaks. The fish chowder can't be beat, either.

St. David's Lighthouse has been seen from an 18-mile radius since its first light in 1879. Made of Bermuda limestone, the structure is only half as high as Gibbs Hill (55 feet) and some 280 feet above sea level. It offers visitors a panoramic view of the eastern end of Bermuda, including the three-island area that is now one (Longbird, St. David's, and Cooper's islands), the dramatic open sea, and the five-mile-square Castle Harbour with its fascinating chain of islands across the entrance. These strangely shaped islands almost link Cooper's to the tip of Tucker's Town, which is also part of St. George's Parish. It is also possible to see from here how sentimental the St. David's folk must be, as one looks down on Annie's Bay, Ruth's Bay and Dolly's Bay. Smaller, but still in evidence, is Emily's Bay. Those must have been some women!

Leaving the rugged beauty of St. David's Island and environs, one passes again the U.S. Naval Air Station and Carter House, skirts around Bermuda's Airport and over the causeway into Hamilton Parish. Follow the Harrington Sound Road into Tucker's Town, which is also part of St. George's Parish even though it was founded in 1616 by Governor Daniel Tucker who wished to abandon St. George's and build a new town on the shore of Castle Harbour. Apparently some streets were laid out and a few cottages built, but the scheme was never a success and Tucker's Town became a small, rather unprosperous community that lived by farming, fishing and whaling. (Whaling was one of the colony's most important industries in the late 18th century and it centered around this eastern end of the islands. Even today it is not unusual to see small cottages with whalebone decorations on front gates.)

For 300 years, Tucker's Town remained a quiet and undeveloped area and, to say the least, unfashionable. But all this changed in the 1920s when Furness Withy & Co., which ran steamships to and from Bermuda full of wealthy passengers, bought a large piece of the area for a splendid golf course and club. The Tucker's Town boom began as members of the exclusive Mid-Ocean Club decided to build residences nearby. The golf course is considered one of the finest around anywhere, with splendid views from every hole, and the club has played host to world statesmen for high-level conferences. No one can buy a house in the area who is not already a member of the Mid-Ocean Club, and private residences have been known to sell recently for over $2 million!

Below the club and the golf course on the south shore are the Natural Arches, probably Bermuda's most photographed natural beauty. They are also among the island's oldest attractions and have been popular for picnics long before the land above became elegant. These spectacular rock formations must be the result of the surf pounding for centuries against caves along the shore. In addition to this beautiful beach, the area has other lovely spots along the south shore as well as in Tucker's Town Bay and Castle Harbour. The same Furness and Withy steamship people also built the fabulous Castle Harbour Hotel on the other side of Tucker's Town, just across the boundary into Hamilton Parish.

Castle Island was once connected to Castle Point, the farthest part of Tucker's Town. Governor Moore built his best fort on this island in the years 1612 and onward, since this one was built of stone. As mentioned before, the governor was worried about invasions from the Spaniards and it was from this fort that the only Spanish attack was repulsed. In 1614 the two Spanish ships were sighted just outside the channel into Castle Harbour. Two shots were fired from the fort; fortunately, this scared the intruders so that they fled to the open sea. According to the history books, this fort had only one cannon ball left, and the early settlers could only assume that Someone above was watching over them. The fort on this island was so fortuitously placed that it was constantly improved over the centuries and even saw active duty during World War II. Only the ruins remain now and the old stones have many interesting tales to tell.

This mid-day scene from the terrace of Cambridge Beaches, the island's oldest cottage colony, depicts Bermuda's serenity and charm.

Bermudian architecture is a 300-year-old tradition. Above, historic St. Peter's Church, with its native cedar doors, stands on the site of the oldest Anglican church in the Western Hemisphere. Below, cottages at the famous Elbow Beach Hotel are built in similar style.

A turquoise sea and delicately-colored sand are part of the attraction of Bermuda's beaches.

Clear skies and crystal waters invite both swimmers and sailors.

Below, vacationers find that motor bikes are an easy way to tour the island.

WHAT TO SEE AND DO

A Practical Guide to Enjoying Bermuda

It is not possible to be bored in Bermuda for this lovely island in the Atlantic has an annual calendar of events to entice visitors to return again and again. There is a super-abundance of activities from which to chose—interesting sights to see, beautiful beaches to relax upon, active and spectator sports, annual festivals and tours, and colorful ceremonies that have been tradition for three centuries.

Bermuda Rendezvous Time. Visitors during Bermuda's "winter season" (December 1, 1981 to March 15, 1982) will not only find the weather perfect for golf and tennis but also a weekly program of free events to entertain them. These include a local craft show, military ceremonies, and a personal welcome to the old town of St. George by its mayor. All events are compliments of the Bermuda government and chamber of commerce.

Monday: A Date with History. A day in the 17th-century town of St. George when the mayor personally greets visitors at 11 A.M. in King's Square, accompanied by the town crier. Members of the Bermuda National Trust take visitors on a walking tour of the old town, relating bits and pieces of history along the way. At noon, gunners from nearby St. Catherine fire the "Noonday Gun" and there is complimentary transportation to the fort.

Tuesday: Bermuda Crafts. The minister of tourism and members of the Chamber of Commerce invite visitors to Pier One in the afternoon to see a variety of local crafts on display and sale—silver, cedar, raffia, cane, plastics, sea shells—and have a complimentary draft beer at "The Pickled Onion," an English pub set up there.

THINGS TO SEE AND DO

1 ALBUOY'S POINT*
2 AQUARIUM, MUSEUM, & ZOO
3 ARBORETUM
4 BERMUDA HISTORICAL SOCIETY MUSEUM*
5 BERMUDA LIBRARY*
6 BERMUDA MARITIME MUSEUM●
7 BERMUDA POTTERY
8 BLUE GROTTO DOLPHINS
9 BOTANICAL GARDENS & CAMDEN
10 BRIDGE HOUSE*●
11 CABINET BUILDING*
12 CARRIAGE MUSEUM*
13 CATHEDRAL*
14 CITY HALL & ART GALLERY*
15 CONFEDERATE MUSEUM*●
16 CRYSTAL CAVES
17 DELIVERANCE*
18 DEVIL'S HOLE
19 EDMUND GIBBONS NATURE RESERVE●
20 FEATHERBED ALLEY PRINTING PRESS*
21 FERRY LANDING*
22 FORT ALBERT
23 FORT HAMILTON*
24 FORT SCAUR
25 FORT ST. CATHERINE
26 GATES FORT
27 GIBBS HILL LIGHT HOUSE
28 GLADYS MORRELL NATURE PRESERVE●
29 GUNPOWDER CAVERN*
30 KING EDWARD VII HOSPITAL
31 LEAMINGTON CAVE
32 NORTH NATURE RESERVE●
33 OLD DEVONSHIRE CHURCH

34 OLD RECTORY*●
35 OLD STATE HOUSE*
36 PAGET MARSH●
37 PALM GROVE GARDEN
38 PAR-LA-VILLE GARDENS*
39 PERFUME FACTORY
40 PEROT POST OFFICE*
41 RABBIT ISLAND●
42 ST. DAVID'S LIGHTHOUSE
43 ST. GEORGE HISTORICAL SOCIETY*
44 ST. GEORGE LIBRARY*●
45 ST. PETER'S CHURCH*
46 SCAUR LODGE PROPERTY●
47 SESSIONS HOUSE & SUPREME COURT*
48 SOMERS GARDEN*
49 SPITTAL POND & SPANISH ROCK●
50 SPRINGFIELD LIBRARY●
51 TOWN HALL*
52 TUCKER HOUSE*●
53 UNFINISHED CATHEDRAL*
54 VERDMONT●
55 VICTORIA PARK*
56 VISITOR'S SERVICE BUREAU, HAMILTON*
57 VISITOR'S SERVICE BUREAU ST. GEORGE*
58 WATERVILLE●
59 CARTER HOUSE
60 SOMER'S WHARF*

● *BERMUDA NATIONAL TRUST PROPERTIES*
* *NUMBER REFERS TO DETAIL MAPS ON OVERLEAF*

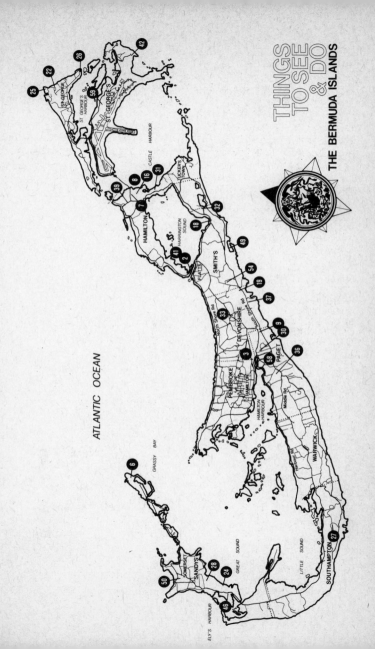

THINGS
TO SEE
& DO

THE BERMUDA ISLANDS

ATLANTIC OCEAN

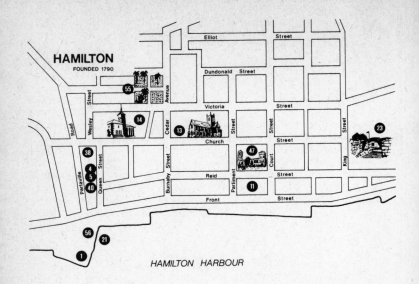

HAMILTON
FOUNDED 1790

Elliot Street

Dundonald Street

Victoria Street

Church Street

Reid Street

Front Street

Wesley Street

Cedar Avenue

Court Street

King Street

Burnaby Street

Parliment Street

Parsaville Street

Queen Street

55

14

13

47

23

38

4

5

40

11

56

21

1

HAMILTON HARBOUR

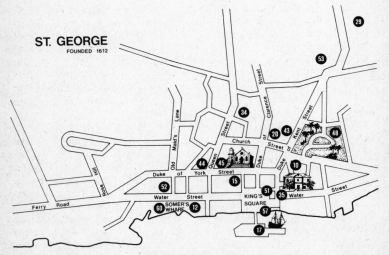

ST. GEORGE
FOUNDED 1612

29

53

Clarence Street

Church Street

Duke of Clarence Street

Kent Street

Old Maid's Lane

Queen Street

York Street

Duke of York Street

Water Street

Rose Hill

Ferry Road

SOMER'S WHARF

KING'S SQUARE

Duke of Clarence Street

Water Street

34

20

43

48

44

45

10

15

52

51

35

60

12

57

17

ST. GEORGE'S HARBOUR

Wednesday: Crossroads of the Atlantic. At noon, kilted pipers and drummers perform the skirling ceremony at Fort Hamilton. Afterward, visitors are encouraged to take a walking tour of the capital city, and shop.

Thursday: Treasure Island. This is the day to visit the rustic village of Somerset by motorbike, taxi, or ferryboat. See the *Maritime Museum* in the Keepyard of the former Royal Naval Dockyard, stop on the way at *Gibbs Hill Lighthouse* in Southampton, see the beaches and the smallest drawbridge in the world. And don't forget the Witch Hunt held at Fort Scaur.

Friday: Golf Tournament. At Bermuda's government golf course, *Port Royal,* designed by Robert Trent Jones, join the weekly Rendezvous Golf Tournament. Registration and further information available at the Golf Clubhouse in Southampton. For those fond of flowers, there is a guided tour of the *Botanical Gardens in Paget,* which leaves at 10:30 A.M. from Il Chianti Restaurant on the property.

Saturday: Festival Day. The festival opens in King's Square, St. George's, with the town crier introducing the Howard Lee Trio while the mayor greets visitors in the Town Hall. Following the trio music, the famous Bermuda Gombeys perform.

Bermuda Festival '82. From mid-January to end of February, Bermuda will hold her fifth annual *International Arts Festival.* Theater, dance, opera, classical and modern music are offered. Performances are held in City Hall, the Anglican Cathedral and Southampton Princess Hotel. Participating past artists included British jazz stars Cleo Laine and Johnny Dankworth, French pianist Philippe Endremont, the Julliard Theatre Group, the New York City Opera company, the Brandenberg Ensemble and the Ballet Repertory company.

Bermuda College Weeks. From March 14 to April 10, 1982, college students from all over will descend upon Bermuda for fun, frolic, and a host of government-sponsored activities. College Weeks began as Rugby Weeks about 40 years ago, when Ivy League rugby teams came to Bermuda to spend their spring holidays and compete against Bermudian and British teams. The girls soon found out where the boys were—and that was the end of serious rugby competition! College Weeks are an annual spring event and the Bermuda government organizes and pays for all of the coeducational activities. All a coed needs is an Identification Card from school, a return ticket, and written confirmation of accommodations. (This should include the name of hotel or cottage, meals included in the rate, number of beds per room, and name of travel agent for whom the group organizer worked.) Upon presentation of the school ID, each student receives a College Week Courtesy Card that entitles him or her to the daily free activities.

Each week begins Sunday evening with a Get Acquainted dance at one of the major hotels (jacket and tie usually required for the gentlemen). On Monday from 10:30 A.M. (should anyone dare to rise so early), a big bash begins at Elbow Beach with lots of fun in the sun, a complimentary lunch, and entertainment by the Bermuda Strollers, a local group. Another beach party is held on Tuesday, with buffet luncheon, swimming, and the Bermuda Limbo Dancers. The College Week cruise aboard the *Canima* takes place on Wednesday from 10:30 A.M. to 1:30 P.M. Complimentary lunch is served on board during the two-hour cruise through the islands of Hamilton Harbour and the Great Sound. Thursday is a free day (often another cruise to accommodate the overflow), and Friday features a steel band concert on yet another beach. A great time is had by all!

Annual Championship Dog Shows. In February, May and November, the *Botanical Gardens* are host to every canine from Rhodesian Ridgebacks to Dandie Dinmont Terriers. The dog shows are sponsored by the All Breed Club of Bermuda.

Art Exhibitions. The exhibition of works by local and foreign artists is sponsored each month at the *Hamilton City Hall Art Gallery* by the Bermuda Society of Arts. The gallery is open from 10:30 A.M. to 4:30 P.M., Monday through Saturday.

Agricultural Exhibition. Every April, the *Botanical Gardens* take on the appearance of a state fair, with horse shows, culinary exhibits, displays of local crafts, flowers, fruits and vegetables and livestock. The show attracts thousands of spectators each spring.

Homes and Gardens Tours. Bermudians open their homes and gardens to visitors during this annual tour sponsored by the *Garden Club of Bermuda*. For a donation of $5, visitors can see a different set of three homes each Wednesday between 2 P.M. to 5 P.M. (rain or shine) from mid-March to mid-May. Tickets are on sale for each day's group at all houses and club volunteers act as hostesses imparting charm and information. The tours raise money for the club's scholarship fund.

Peppercorn Ceremony. This colorful ceremony has been a tradition since 1816 when the State House (the seat of Bermuda government from 1620 to 1815 when the capital moved to Hamilton) was granted to the mayor, aldermen and common council of St. George in trust for a Masonic Lodge for the annual rent of one peppercorn.

The date for the annual payment of rent was originally the 27th of December (the Feast of St. John the Evangelist) but was changed to the most suitable day nearest the 23rd of April, St. George's Day, in honor of the Patron Saint from whom the ancient town derives its name. (It will take place on April 21, 1982.)

On the day of the Peppercorn Ceremony, the regular meeting of Her Majesty's Executive Council in Bermuda (normally held in the Council Chambers in Hamilton) is held in the State House. The governor of Bermuda arrives in a horse-drawn carriage with much pomp and plumage, is welcomed by the mayor of St. George, and receives a key to the State House for the purpose of holding this meeting and upholding conditions of this lease. The key is turned over, the rent is delivered on a velvet pillow, and the members of the Executive Council proceed to the State House for their meeting. Members of the Bermuda Regiment carry the Colours (banners) presented to them by Princess Margaret in 1965.

Ceremony of Beating Retreat. This ceremony, which dates from 16th-century British military history, can be viewed on Front Street in Hamilton, Kings Square in St. George, and Somerset Cricket Field. It is performed by the pipes and drums of the Bermuda Regiment and the Bermuda Cadet Pipe Band. Members of the band wear the Gordon Kilt and some are as young as 13 years of age.

Bermuda Heritage Week. Begun only in 1979, the week from May 18 to 24 is a week of cultural activities to celebrate Bermuda's heritage. There are thanksgiving services in historic churches around the island, youth music performances, cultural evenings and a heritage exhibition. The week of activity culminates with a festival parade from Hamilton City Hall on May 24th, Bermuda Day.

Bermuda Day. (Formerly *Commonwealth Day*). May 24th is a public holiday and the day Bermudians traditionally head for the beaches for their first swim of the year. It also marks the beginning of the fitted dinghy racing season in St. George's Harbour. And if this is not enough, there is a half-marathon (about 13 miles) race from the Somerset Cricket Club to the National Stadium in Devonshire.

Queen's Birthday Parade. A military parade takes place on Front Street in Hamilton each year to celebrate the queen's official birthday. The parade is scheduled for June 12 in 1982 and places of business will be closed on Monday, June 14.

Convening of Parliament. The governor drives up every year in October in the state landau, pulled by a pair of black beauties, to open Parliament. He is dressed for the occasion in full regalia, with a plumed hat, and joined by the British Regiment.

BERMUDA NATIONAL TRUST. This non-profit organization, founded in 1970 to watch over the island's open spaces and historic buildings, sponsors an annual walk every Palm Sunday (April 4, 1982) to take visitors and residents through scenic parts of Bermuda not normally seen. The Trust is proprietor of 21 buildings and over 60 acres of open space, all open to the public. The open spaces are:

North Nature Reserve (Mangrove Lake, Smith's Parish). Situated on the western end of the lake, just across the road from Pink Beach, is an area of living mangroves growing in a brackish (salty) pond. The pond itself is fascinating to students of water flora and fauna and attracts several species of birds.

Spittal Pond (South Road, Smith's Parish). This is the most spectacular of the Trust's open spaces and Bermuda's largest wildlife sanctuary. On this nearly 60 acres, approximately 25 different species of waterfowl come to visit between November and May.

Edmund Gibbons Nature Reserve (South Shore Road, Devonshire Parish). Situated just west of the junction with Collector's Hill, this portion of marshland provides living space for a number of birds and rare species of Bermuda flora.

Paget Marsh (Middle Road, Paget). Special arrangements are necessary to visit this 18 acres of unspoiled wood and marsh land which contains vegetation of ecological interest. Please call Trust headquarters (2-6483) during the morning for permission.

Scaur Lodge Property (Somerset Road, Somerset, Sandys Parish). This open area includes the site of Scaur Lodge, a Bermuda cottage severely damaged by waterspout which came up on land, turned into a tornado and drove across this neck of Somerset Island. The property is typical of Bermuda's steeply rising shoreline hillside.

Gladys Morrell Nature Reserve (East Shore Road, Sandys Parish near Cavello Bay). Two acres of open space donated by Daughters of the Empire.

Springfield and Gilbert Nature Reserve (Somerset Road, Somerset, Sandys Parish). Springfield, an old plantation home, adjoins the Gilbert Nature Reserve, which was part of the land attached to the house. The building is fascinating from an architectural point of view and the nature reserve consists of five acres of unspoiled woodland, open space and planting land. The finest rooms in the house are the Somerset branch of the Bermuda Library but are only open Mondays and Wednesday from 10 A.M. to 6 P.M. (closed from 1 P.M. to 2 P.M.) and Saturdays from 10 A.M. to 5 P.M.

Prize of the historic homes and buildings owned by the Bermuda National Trust is **Verdmont** (Collector's Hill, Smith's Parish), a fine 17th-century Bermuda mansion, containing antique furniture, china and portraits. The cedar stair balustrade is considered to be the finest on the island. Open weekdays from 10 A.M. to 5 P.M. (except lunch interval). Admission fee is $1.

Tucker House (Water Street, St. George's) is the historic home of an early and distinguished member of the Tucker family of England, Bermuda and Virginia. There is a fine collection of Bermuda furniture, silver and portraits as well as the Joseph Rainey Memorial Room where the first black member of the U.S. House of Representatives practiced barbering as a refugee during the American Civil War. Open weekdays from 10 A.M. to 5 P.M. Admission fee is $1.

Confederate Museum in Globe Hotel (The Square, St. George's). The former Globe Hotel (1698) was the headquarters of the principal Southern agent in Bermuda, concerned with procurement and blockade running during the American Civil War. The museum houses an interesting collection of exhibits from this period. Open weekdays from 10 A.M. to 5 P.M. Admission is 50¢.

The Old Rectory (Broad Alley, St. George's). This is a charming old Bermuda Cottage built about 1705 by a reformed pirate. Open Tuesdays and Saturdays from 10 A.M. to 5 P.M. (except lunch interval). No admission fee.

Stuart Hall (Queen Street, St. George's). Stuart Hall was built about 1706 and is now used as the St. George's branch of the Bermuda Public Library. Open Monday and Wednesday from 10 A.M. to 6 P.M. (closed from 1 P.M. to 2 P.M.); Saturdays from 10 A.M. to 5 P.M. No admission fee.

Bermuda Maritime Museum (Dockyard, Sandys). In the fortified Keepyard of the former Royal Navy Dockyard, this impressive museum provides an opportunity to follow Bermuda's seagoing heritage as well as a massive fortress designed to protect the British fleet in Bermuda waters. Open daily from 10 A.M. to 5 P.M. Admission for adults is $1, children under 12 years are 50¢.

Crafts shops are being operated in two interesting Trust buildings which are worth a visit both for the crafts and the buildings themselves. Mrs. Jill Raine operates the **Bridge House Art Gallery** (Bridge Street, just off the square in St. George's) selling her own ceramic jewelry and the works of other Bermuda artists. **Winterhaven Farm Cottage** (Harrington Sound Road at Devil's Hole, Smith's Parish), has been sold to a real estate firm and is no longer a National Trust property or open to the public.

Any questions about the properties can be addressed to the Bermuda National Trust, "Waterville", Paget (tel: 2-6483), where the director, William Zuill, sits in a cluttered office surrounded by a bevy of ducks and swans in the backyard. The whole scene is only fitting for an organization that cares so tenderly for Bermuda's historic property and open places.

 SPECTATOR SPORTS. Bermudians are what one might call "sporting" and there are any number of sport events to keep visitors on the go throughout the year. For those who prefer to be spectators, there are soccer matches every weekend from September through May. Rugby and field hockey are regular fixtures on Thursdays, Saturdays and Sundays from September through April. Cricket is the summer spectator sport, highlighted by the annual *Cup Match Cricket Festival* in late July. Watching the cricket competition between teams from the eastern and western ends of the island is only one reason Bermudians and visitors alike head for the Cup Match. It's also a time to show off new clothes and perhaps win a little money at the crown-and-anchor tables during the most colorful of Bermuda's sporting events.

Sailing: Races are held every Saturday from the end of January through the fall season by the *Royal Bermuda Yacht Club* in a variety of classes including Solings, International One-Designs, Luders-16s, 5-0-5s, Lasers, etc. The *Bermuda Offshore Cruising Association* holds races on the first Sunday of each month for ocean-going yachts. The beautiful Bermuda-fitted dinghies race approximately every other Sunday during the spring, summer and fall, starting on May 24th in St. George's and Hamilton harbors and in Mangrove Bay, Sandys. Visitors frequently compete in Sunfish races on Harrington Sound each Sunday.

The spectacular *Newport to Bermuda Yacht Race* is held in mid-June every even year while the *Newport to Bermuda Multihull Race* is held on the odd year. The yacht race is the more glamorous and exciting, and draws serious sailors and their elegant boats from all over the world. When the yachts reach Bermuda, there are plenty of parties to fete the victor and console the losers.

Powerboat races take place on Sundays from May through November at Ferry Reach, near the airport. Closed-circuit races alternate with offshore races. Marathons with top international drivers teaming up with local drivers are held periodically, and the *Around the Island race* is usually held in August.

Annual Game Fishing Tournament: The Bermuda Department of Tourism offers certificates and sterling silver pins for top catches of 17 varieties of game fish found in local waters. The tournament is open to visitors from May through November. No license and no entry fee required.

In July, an invitational event draws teams from the U.S. and other countries for four days of competition against each other and a variety of tackle-busting fish.

Annual Goodwill Golf Tournament: This tournament in early December attracts some 100 American, Canadian, and British pro-amateur foursomes. During the winter season, there are many other golf tournaments sponsored by local clubs and resorts (see *Sports* section).

Coral Beach Invitational Tennis Championships: This tournament is held in November at the Coral Beach and Tennis Club, which sponsors it. There are also weekly tournaments at many hotels for their guests (see *Sports* section).

Bermuda Fourth Annual International Marathon: This 26-mile, 385-yard endurance race is scheduled for January 31, 1982. Sponsored by the Bermuda Department of Tourism, Eastern Airlines and Puma, the sports equipment people. This marathon is beginning to attract "name" runners, but everyone is invited to join. There is a 10 kilometer race the day before (January 30). Anyone wishing to enter the race may write to: President, Bermuda Track & Field Assoc., P.O. Box 397, Devonshire, Bermuda.

 BOTANICAL GARDENS. Even people who don't like botanical gardens will enjoy these 36 acres of tended gardens. Every indigenous plant found on the island is here as well as thousands that have been imported. Stroll through the lush landscape and have lunch or dinner at Il Chianti. Permanent attractions are the Garden for the Blind, Hibiscus Garden, Palm Garden, Cacti and Succulent Garden and more. Free tours are conducted from 10:30 A.M. to noon on Tuesday, Wednesday and Friday (except public holidays). The gardens are open daily from sunrise to sunset and the plant houses can be visited from 8 A.M. to 5 P.M. (except public holidays), Monday through Saturday. Admission is free.

FORTS. Cruise passengers aboard vessels entering the principal channel of the island get their first view of *Fort St. Catherine*. The stone fortification was built in the 19th century on the site of a wooden construction that dated from 1612. The first governor of Bermuda, Richard Moore, built nine forts at strategic places to prevent invasion from the free-roving Spaniards. Unfortunately, eight of them were wood and did not last but the sites he chose were so accurate that stone fortifications were built upon them later.

Fort St. Catherine has been fully restored and its underground galleries are used to highlight the island's early history while a replica of the Crown Jewels can be viewed in one of the upper galleries. The fort is one of Bermuda's most popular tourist attractions. It is open from 10 A.M. to 4:30 P.M. and adult admission is $1.

The one stone fortification that Governor Moore built was *King's Fort* on Castle Island, to guard the entrance to Castle Harbour. Shots were fired from this fort at a Spanish warship in 1614 and she fortuitously fled after two rounds, because Moore's men had only one shot left! (It is now in ruins.)

In 1834, the famous Duke of Wellington (who had defeated Napoleon at Waterloo) devised a scheme for the defense of this little island which included the building of *Fort Scaur* in Somerset, *Fort Hamilton* overlooking the capital city, and the South Shore Road. Wellington's plan was to station troops all along this road to protect the South Shore but there was never a need.

The restored *Fort Hamilton* offers a panoramic view of the city and harbor. Its old cannons still point threateningly out at sea and its musty labyrinth of galleries are open. One enters the fort from a wooden bridge that crosses the moat now filled with native flora. Walk around the moat and feel that you are in a jungle of exotic plants and birds. The fort is open from 9:30 A.M. to 5 P.M. Sunday through Friday (*closed Saturday*) and approached via Victoria and King Streets and Happy Valley Road. The timid should taxi up and walk down.

Fort Scaur in Somerset has also been restored and offers a view of the Great Sound. Open from 9 A.M. to 5 P.M. daily, it is a good place to rest and picnic on a day's jaunt by motorbike to the westward end of the island. Sit on the grassy knoll and enjoy the sun. You will probably be asked to sign the guestbook.

Gates Fort, on the island of St. George's, was also built between 1612 and 1615 under the direction of Governor Moore. It was named after Sir Thomas Gates, one of the prominent persons aboard the shipwrecked *Sea Venture*, who is said to have leapt ashore and shouted, "This is Gates, his Bay!" This smaller, also restored fort is open from 9 A.M. to 5 P.M. daily.

 CHURCHES. There are plenty of charming churches to visit throughout the island and their graveyards are a fascinating course in history. (Do not hesitate to stop and wander through each one.) *St. Peter's* (Duke of York Street, St. George's) is the oldest church in Bermuda and stands on the oldest site in continuous use of an Anglican church in the Western Hemisphere. It is a simple, whitewashed building with highly polished cedar doors, floors and pews. Its pulpit and altar date from the early 17th century and the font is believed to be 15th century. The communion service was presented by King William III and the walls are lined with memorial tablets to well-known Bermudian names. The graveyard behind the building is also full of famous names, including U.S. Consul John W. Howden who died of yellow fever in 1852 (his tombstone says, "We Shall Meet Again"), a young American seaman Richard Sutherland Dale who died in the last, and futile, battle of the War of 1812, and Sir Richard Sharples and his aide, Captain Hugh Sayers, who were assassinated on the grounds of Government House in 1973.

Not far from St. George's is the stone ruin of a church that never quite made it. Known as the *Unfinished Cathedral*, it has its own majesty and history even though it lies abandoned with only the palm trees for company.

Bermuda's Anglican Cathedral, on Church Street in Hamilton, was dedicated in 1894 but built in early English style. It is a bright and cheerful church, with beautiful stained-glass windows that shine even on a dull day. One of them, the Angel Window on the east wall, was designed by a local artist, Vivienne Gilmore Gardener. A Warrior Chapel, dedicated in 1977, contained the flags of the armed forces connected with Bermuda, and two throne chairs for use on royal occasions. The kneeling pads in the pews are all hand-embroidered and add a personal touch to the long nave.

 LIGHTHOUSES. *Gibbs Hill Lighthouse* is one of the few lighthouses in the world made of cast iron, which had been cast in England and brought to the island in pieces. On May 1, the lighthouse will celebrate its 133rd birthday and the light, which shines some 354 feet above sea level, can be seen by sailors as far away as 40 miles. The light is supplied by a 1500-watt electric bulb (installed in 1952) and the perfectly polished brass mechanism that circulates the beam can be seen by climbing 185 steps up. If it's a clear day, it's also a good way to see forever! If it's windy, the timid should remain below because this lighthouse does have a reputation for swaying. Open 9 A.M. to 4:30 P.M. daily. Admission over 3 years of age is 50¢.

St. David's Lighthouse celebrates its 101st anniversary this year. Located at St. David's Island in St. George's Parish, this stone structure is half the size of Gibbs Hill but equally important to ships entering the main channel. Unfortunately, it is no longer open to the public.

CAVES. Four of Bermuda's fascinating caves, a subterranean world full of stalagmites and stalactites and mirror lakes, are open to the public. Well worth the tour are *Crystal Cave* and *Leamington Cave* in Bailey's Bay, which attract thousands of visitors each year. The former was discovered by two young boys in 1907, a two-acre cavern with a tidal pool that is 200 feet long and as much as 80 feet deep. A bridge was built in the cave in 1928 and now visitors can walk along while colored lights dance against the ice formations. Leamington Cave, which was discovered in 1910 and opened to the public four years later, is not far away. Both cost $1.50 for adults and tours are available daily. *Crystal Caves* is open from 9 A.M. to 5 P.M. and *Leamington Caves* is open from 9 A.M. to 4:30 P.M. but closed from January 15 to March 1.

The Grotto Bay Beach and Tennis Club has turned one of its caves into a swinging nightclub. Called *Prospero's Cave and Discotheque*, the cave features seating for 80 persons around an underground lake that is 25 feet deep in some places. Next to it is *Cathedral Cave* and the hotel offers tours on Wednesday and Saturday at 10 A.M., but be forewarned—you may have to crawl along. If you are an avid spelunker, you will revel in this sort of thing but wear old clothes and cover your knees!

HISTORIC SITES. A replica of the *Deliverance*, one of the two ships built by the castaways from the *Sea Venture* in 1609, can be visited daily on Ordnance Island, St. George's, from 10 A.M. to 5 P.M. The original *Deliverance* was 80 tons and built from salvage from the wreck of the *Sea Venture* plus cedar found on the island. It carried 130 people. This *Deliverance*, commissioned by the Bermuda Junior Service League, was planned by a local marine enthusiast and finished in 1971 at a cost of $110,000. It is open daily from 10 A.M. to 5 P.M. and adult admission is 50¢ .

Carter House, one of Bermuda's oldest stone structures, has been restored and is open to the public (free) on Wednesdays and Fridays from 10 A.M. to 2 P.M. The cottage, located in St. David's, was built around 1640 by Christopher Carter, one of the original crew of the *Sea Venture*. Passes to view this historical landmark must be obtained at the U.S. Naval Air Station (Gate 1) on St. David's Island.

Carriage Museum: The automobile only came to Bermuda in 1946 and suddenly, the horse-drawn carriage became a thing of the past. Many of these fine, custom-built vehicles were saved and in 1960 put into a museum that is one of the most fun places on the whole island. In it are a Surrey with fringe on top, a Brougham, Semi-Formal Phaeton, a Hearse built in 1856 for St. George's and used for over a century, a Victoria that came from the Metropolitan Opera House in Philadelphia but saw 30 years active service in Bermuda, a Buck-board, Pony Cart, Dog Cart and more. The curator will let you climb into the carriages to dream of bygone days and will even insist upon taking your photo. Just focus your camera and let him push the button—it's fun to see when you get home. The Carriage Museum on Somer's Wharf in St. George's is open Monday through Saturday from 9 A.M. to 5 P.M. Admission is a worthy $1.

Perot Post Office, Bermuda Library, Par-La-Ville Gardens: Just a short skip from the ferry landing, around the policeman's "birdcage" and up Queen Street, is Hamilton's first post office, named after William Bennett Perot, the first postmaster. Next door to the post office was Perot's home, now the Bermuda Library and the gardens that he nurtured are now a public park. An historical museum on the ground floor of this two-story building has exhibits of old cedar furniture, china, hog pennies (the original money of the island) as well as portraits of Sir George and Lady Somers, a copy of the 17th-century map made by Richard Norwood who surveyed the islands and divided them into the tribes they are today, as well as a copy of the letter George Washington wrote from Camp Cambridge on September 6, 1775 to beg the islanders for gunpowder to fight the British. Perot Post Office is open from 8 A.M. to 5 P.M. Monday through Friday, to 12 noon on Saturday (buy some colorful stamps) and the Historical Society Museum is open from 10 A.M. to 5 P.M. Monday through Saturday (except Thursday and lunch interval). Both are free for the browsing and a bit of reliving history.

Maritime Museum: Located in the former Royal Navy Dockyard, Ireland Island, in Somerset, the Maritime Museum has an impressive exhibition of Bermuda's seagoing history of over 300 years. A self-guided tour begins in the Queen's Exhibition Hall, originally built in 1850 to store gunpowder, through other massive stone buildings to the Keepyard with its figure of Neptune taken from the old battleship H.M.S. *Irresistible,* to the gun emplacements and magazines that surround the entire dockyard. A large building on the upper level is the former home of the commissioner of the Dockyard and a fine example of British colonial architecture. It is at present "off limits" but eventual restoration is planned. This indoor-outdoor museum is full of ship models as well as fascinating fixtures taken from them. The eastern building houses the Bermuda Fitted Dinghy exhibit, including the 17-foot *Spirit of Bermuda* built by two local men in 1935 to sail to New York. Plan to spend plenty of time here—it's worth it! Treasure House is the museum's newest and oldest addition (it was originally built in 1849). Completely restored, it now houses the valuable Tucker Treasure and is also the home of diving exhibits. The Maritime Museum is open daily from 10 A.M. to 5 P.M. Adult admission is $2, children under 12 pay 50¢.

OTHER ATTRACTIONS. The *Bermuda Aquarium, Museum and Zoo* is located in Flatt's Village, North Shore Road, Hamilton Parish. Here you can see all forms of the island's tropical marine life, natural history and an amusing collection of parrots, flamingo and giant tortoise that come from the Galapagos Islands in the Pacific. A new exhibit depicts Bermuda's geological development in relation to the rest of the world. Open daily from 9 A.M. to 5 P.M. Admission is $2 for adults, 50¢ for children under 12 years of age.

Devil's Hole in Harrington Sound is a protected pool where you can fish but can't catch anything. It is billed as Bermuda's "first attraction" since the original owner, Mr. Trott, began charging visitors an admission fee since 1843. Open Monday through Saturday from 9 A.M. to 5 P.M. (Sundays and holidays from 10 A.M. to 5 P.M.), adult admission is $1.75, children are $1.

Children and the young at heart will also enjoy the Blue Grotto Dolphins that perform five times daily in a beautiful setting on *Blue Hole Hill* in Hamilton Parish. Admission is $2.50 for adults, $1.00 for children from 4 to 12 years.

SHOPPING. The best way to come to Bermuda is with a half-empty suitcase. While there may be few bargains left in the world, there are certainly good buys in the colony, especially on

British imports. Woolens, china and crystal are all about 30 percent less than in the U.S. and there are no sales taxes to worry about. Liquor is also much less but only sold duty-free in five packs so you do end up paying some duty on it when returning to the U.S. (Check with local state laws on the importation of liquor and cigarettes.)

You do not have to walk very far to spend your money as most of the well-known shops are located along a three-block area of Front Street. Here you will find *Trimingham's*, which has been a tradition since 1844 and full of classic British woolens for the whole family, jewelry, perfumes, accessories, china and crystal, art work, antiques and furnishings for the home. The pumpkin-colored Trimmingham's will not accept any credit cards but will use them as identification to open up a personal charge account for you. A bill for your purchases will be sent to your home about a month or so later, along with instructions on how much postage is necessary to insure airmail. It's a very civilized way of doing business.

If you can't find what you want at Trimmy's, the clerk will probably suggest that you go next door to *Smith's*, which has the same type of merchandise (accepts American Express credit cards). Smith's has a fine collection of perfumes, china and crystal, and British woolens including its very own Bermuda Blue Plaid, one of the most attractive tartans made. Buy it in skirts, slacks, scarfs, handbags or in yard goods.

A.S. Cooper is another local department store full of British imports including Jaeger apparel at great savings over U.S. prices. One sweater certainly leads to another and there are plenty of shops around that sell them. In addition to the larger stores mentioned, *The English Sports Shop* is located on Front Street and in the larger hotels, and the *Crown Colony Shop* has a good selection. For fine china and crystal and an upstairs full of antiques, *Bluck's* can't be beat and will deliver large packages to your hotel or ship. The china and crystal comes from all over the world and is beautifully chosen and displayed. Bluck's stocks several patterns of Herend, the popular hand-painted china from Hungary, at prices that are less than half asked in New York stores. They will also order china or crystal for you, but beware, it could take over a year!

Other specialty shops along Front Street are *Archie Brown & Son* (clothing and gifts for the entire family), the *Irish Linen Shop, Calypso* (colorful resort wear and original Haitian oil paintings), and *Cecile* (fashions imported from Italy, France, etc.). *Heritage House* (next to Bluck's) has a large array of gift items and there are several large jewelry shops along Front Street, most of them featuring watches from Japan and Europe. Perfume is another good buy in

Bermuda and one can even take a tour of the *Lili Perfume Factory* in Baileys Bay to see how they make a local brand.

For books, one can't beat *Baxter's Bookshops,* and *Pegasus* has a large selection of Bermuda maps and prints, displayed in an old house near the Hamilton Princess Hotel.

The liquor and wine merchants can all be found in central Hamilton and in branches throughout the island. They sell liquor duty-free only in five-bottle packages, your choice of the five bottles. Although you may save a great deal of money this way, there are Customs duties to pay either when leaving Bermuda by air or upon arrival at a U.S. port. In most of the shops, you may choose the five bottles you want while others offer only a pre-selected package. Delivery of all packages are made direct to ship or plane and under local Customs supervision for this liquor is considered "in bond" in Bermuda.

Locally made products feature carved souvenirs of Bermuda cedar, Bermuda Sherry Peppers (adds spice to soups and stews), fragrances and perfumes, some pottery, Bermuda Gold Liqueur, and works by Bermudian artists. There are also lovely silk screen materials and prints, pressed flowers and plants (Bermudian, of course), candles in all shapes and sizes, straw goods, wooden plaques, and dolls made from plants.

One of the most beloved of Bermudian artists is a charming eccentric named Alfred Birdsey who whips a watercolor together in a few minutes and charges about $20. Birdsey captures the colors and spirit of the island where his family has lived for generations. His son-in-law runs the shop (*Rosecote,* Stowe Hill, Paget) and is now selling reproductions that are as good as the originals.

Anyone with the time to browse should also look at the large selection of imported antiques, ranging from hatpins to dining-room tables, in local shops. Silver, china and furniture can be found in seven large rooms on the top floor of *William Bluck and Company.* Next door is *Heritage Antiques,* run by William Bluck's grandson, Jay Bluck. This store is stocked with Chippendale furniture, cranberry glass, nautical maps and prints, copper buckets and tankards, and Staffordshire figurines.

Trimingham's has a good collection of 19th century oil paintings; and antique maps and early prints are a specialty at the *Pegasus Print and Map Shop* near the Hamilton Princess Hotel, and the *Old Book Cellar* in the basement of President Henry Tucker House in St. George's. At the *Thistle Gallery* on Park Street (behind Hamilton City Hall) are Victorian watercolors, old tea caddies, and sets of hallmarked silver coffee spoons. Here are also old brass pieces, copper, silver and silver plate, and a selection of antique Wedgewood china.

Coin collectors can find old British coinage at the *Bermuda Coin and Stamp Company,* located off Front Street on Old Cellar Lane. Here are also mounted sets of coins and a wide variety of stamps from all over the world.

British antiques over 100 years can be taken into the U.S. duty-free, but Bermudian antiques, especially the beautiful cedar furniture, should not be taken off the island.

SPORTS

Head for the Greens, Nets and Shores

Bermudians love the out-of-doors and are enthusiastic sportsmen. They have built more golf courses per square acre than any other country in the world. They also have more tennis courts, sailboats, racing power boats, fishing facilities, swimming, snorkeling, scuba diving for treasures beneath the sea, riding and, of course, croquet and cricket. If you prefer to "spectate" rather than do it yourself, you will enjoy the annual *Cup Cricket* match in July between the Island's two teams. There are also softball, soccer, lacross, power boat racing, motorcycle scrambling and go-kart racing.

Golf

Tennis and golf are year-round sports on the island and there are plenty of places to play both games. There are a total of nine golf courses spread around the island, three are 9-holers and include the par-three pitch and putt facility at *Horizons Cottage Colony* and the government-owned *Ocean View Golf Course* in Devonshire Parish. Each of the six 18-hole courses offers the player a challenge, with Mid-Ocean Club and the adjacent *Castle Harbour Golf Club* in Tucker's Town providing the toughest as well as the most scenic golf holes on the island. The *Port Royal Golf Course* in Southampton Parish is rated by the pros as the colony's second most challenging course. Port Royal was designed by the famous Robert Trent Jones and is owned and operated by the Bermuda government. There are approximately 13 tournaments "sanctioned" by the Bermuda Golf Association each year, of which eight are held between November and February, the official months for golf. Visitors on golfing holidays will find that the resort hotels hold weekly tournaments for their guests.

Introduction is required at both the *Mid Ocean Club* and *Riddell's Bay Golf Club* but not at *Queen's Park* or *Port Royal.* Hotel courses require advance booking for non-hotel guests as well as starting times for all players. All of the courses have a well-supplied pro shop where equipment can be purchased, and golf clubs are for hire, although not usually in large quantities and not always in a full set. Golf balls can also be bought here as well as in the island's leading stores and cost between $12 to $20 per dozen. Between late September and early November, many courses reseed their greens so it is

GOLF AND TENNIS FACILITIES

GOLF

1 BELMONT HOTEL & GOLF CLUB
2 CASTLE HARBOUR HOTEL & GOLF CLUB
3 HOLIDAY INN HOTEL
4 MID OCEAN CLUB
5 OCEAN VIEW GOLF & COUNTRY CLUB
6 PORT ROYAL GOLF COURSE
7 PRINCESS GOLF CLUB
8 RIDDELL'S BAY GOLF & COUNTRY CLUB

TENNIS

9 STONINGTON BEACH HOTEL
10 ARIEL SANDS
11 BELMONT HOTEL
12 BERMUDIANA HOTEL
13 CAMBRIDGE BEACHES
14 CASTLE HARBOUR HOTEL
15 CORAL BEACH CLUB
16 ELBOW BEACH HOTEL
17 GOVERNMENT TENNIS STADIUM
18 GROTTO BAY HOTEL
19 HARMONY HALL
20 HOLIDAY INN HOTEL
21 HORIZONS & COTTAGES
22 INVERURIE HOTEL
23 LANTANA
24 MID OCEAN CLUB
25 PINK BEACH CLUB
26 POMPANO BEACH CLUB
27 PORT ROYAL TENNIS CLUB
28 THE REEFS
29 HAMILTONIAN HOTEL
30 SONESTA BEACH HOTEL
31 SOUTHAMPTON PRINCESS HOTEL
32 WILLOWBANK

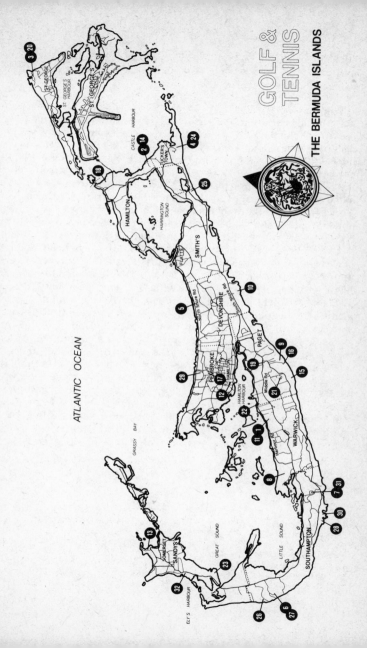

GOLF &
TENNIS

THE BERMUDA ISLANDS

ATLANTIC OCEAN

advisable to check on conditions during this period. Some courses use temporary greens while others keep the original greens in play while reseeding and resurfacing.

Tennis

Enthusiasm for tennis has grown as rapidly in Bermuda as it has in the rest of the world and the number of courts has more than doubled in recent years. Actually, tennis is an old and favored game in the colony, since the first lawn tennis court was built on the grounds of a private home in 1873. A year later, the game was introduced to the United States through Mary Outerbridge who took some equipment and a set of rules to the Staten Island Cricket Club in New York. However, Bermudians boast that the first tennis tournament in the Western Hemisphere took place on their island in 1877. Tennis is a year-round sport here and there are many tournaments throughout the year for both top local and international players.

Currently, there are about 115 courts dotting the landscape, with approximately 85 accessible to visitors. The *Southampton Princess Hotel* provides the largest facility with 11 courts, including 7 that are available for night tennis. The *Government Tennis Stadium*, site of many matches played by ranking world tennis pros, has 8 courts, and the *Coral Beach and Tennis Club* has 7. Both facilities are available for night tennis. The large hotels all have pro shops near their courts where equipment and lessons are available, and racquets are for rent. The larger properties charge both guests and nonguests for the use of courts while others do not charge their own guests (which is as it should be). During the summer season, the best time to play is in the early morning or evening hours. If a sudden rain squall comes, don't worry. Just sweep the water off the courts and they will dry quickly. One final note: Proper tennis clothes are required on all Bermuda courts, with white clothing and shoes preferrable.

PUBLIC BEACHES

1 CHAPLIN BAY	8 LONG BAY BEACH
2 CHURCH BAY	9 SHELLY BAY BEACH
3 DEVONSHIRE BAY	10 STONEHOLE BAY
4 ELBOW BEACH	11 STOVELL BAY
5 HORSESHOE BAY	12 TOBACCO BAY
6 JOBSON'S COVE	13 WARWICK LONG BAY
7 JOHN SMITH'S BAY	14 WEST WHALE BAY

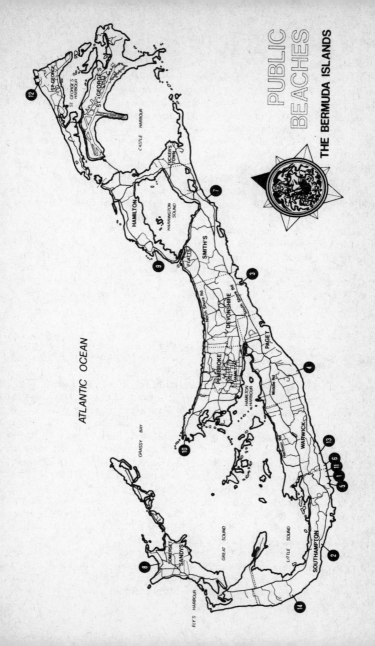

PUBLIC
BEACHES
THE BERMUDA ISLANDS

ATLANTIC OCEAN

ST. GEORGE'S
ST. GEORGE'S HARBOUR
ST. GEORGE'S
CASTLE HARBOUR
TUCKER'S TOWN
HARRINGTON SOUND
HAMILTON
SMITH'S
FLATTS
DEVONSHIRE
North Shore Rd
South Shore Rd
PEMBROKE
PAGET
HAMILTON HARBOUR
Middle Rd
GRASSY BAY
WARWICK
Harbour Rd
SOUTHAMPTON
GREAT SOUND
LITTLE SOUND
SOMERSET
SANDYS
ELY'S HARBOUR

Swimming

Bermuda has some of the most beautiful beaches in the world, with the cream of the crop located along the south shore from Southampton to Tucker's Town. Some are long sweeps of unbroken pink sand while others are divided by low coral cliffs into protected little coves. There are such interesting names as *Horseshoe Bay, Whalebone Bay, Elbow Beach, Jobson's Cove* and *West Whale Bay.* All of these beaches are easily accessible by bicycle or taxi and there are changing facilities in beach clubs along them that are open from mid-March through October. Swimming is enjoyable from about late April to mid-November but the beach season is not officially open for most Bermudians until Bermuda Day (May 24), when local residents traditionally take to the shores.

However, swimming can also be a year-round sport here as there are a certain number of warm days during the winter months when the air temperature is in the 20s C. (70s F.) and the sea temperature rarely drops below the low teen's C. (60s F.). Many hotels and cottage colonies have heated pools and *Sonesta Beach, Bermudiana* and *Southampton Princess* hotels have covered pools which make swimming a year-round pleasure.

Beach Clubs

The three large beach clubs along the south shore all have excellent changing facilities as well as complete luncheon facilities and bar. The *South Shore Beach Club* in Warwick is open daily until 5 P.M. and a locker with towel is available for non-hotel guests *(Belmont, Bermudiana, Harmony Hall)* for about $2 per person. Lunch is available from noon to 4:30 P.M. and the bar is open from 10:30 A.M. to 4 P.M. (from May to August from 11 A.M. to 6:30 P.M.). The *Breakers Club* on John Smith's Bay, Smith's Parish, is open daily from 10:30 A.M. to 1 A.M. Towels and mats are for rent and include use of changing room. Lunch facilities are available from noon to 3:45 P.M. and the bar is open from 11 A.M. to 1 A.M. At the *Elbow Beach Hotel* in Paget, the beach club is open daily until 5 P.M. with lockers and towels provided free to guests. Admission charge for non-guests is about $3 and lounge chairs and umbrellas are for rent. Lunch is available from 12 noon to 2:30 P.M. (sandwiches until 3 P.M.) and the bar is open until 5 P.M.

If you plan to spend a few hours on a beach where there are no changing facilities, wear your swim suit underneath sports clothes if cycling. Bathing suits are not allowed for riding on motorbikes; in case of a fall, the rider is completely unprotected.

Scuba Diving and Snorkeling

Bermuda's clear waters are perfect for such sports as scuba diving, helmet diving and snorkeling. Treasure diving has reached a fine art around the island and the hero is Teddy Tucker who has brought up thousands of dollars of gold and riches from the deep. Tucker's greatest treasure is a gold and emerald cross (valued at $100,000) that was recovered from the Spanish ship *San Pedro*, lost on the north reefs in the fall of 1594. Tucker and his partner, Bob Canton, had also recovered some interesting gold trinkets from the Spanish galleon *San Antonio*, wrecked on September 12, 1621 on the west reefs while en route from Havana to Cadiz. If you are staying at *Cambridge Beaches* in Sandys Parish (near Tucker's home), you will walk on millstones recovered from the English Brig *Caesar*, wrecked west of Bermuda in 1818, and both brought up by Tucker and laid on the terrace of the cottage colony. And if you're visiting the lighthouse on *Gibbs Hill,* you will find some old medicine vials from this same wreckage for sale at giveaway prices.

There are two qualified, certified and government-licensed divers on Bermuda who also cater to the whims of tourists. One of them is *David McLeod* whose *Skin Diving Adventures* are available daily from March to November and one of his favorite venues is over the wreckage of the *Constellation* which plowed into one of the coral reefs to the northwest of the island in 1943. The ship was carrying a full cargo of cement, glassware, cosmetics, medical supplies, and yo-yos, much of which is still 25 feet down on the floor of the sea waiting to be collected by adventurous visitors.

The other is *Kevin Burke* who introduces beginners to the underwater safaris that scuba diving has to offer by putting them first in the swimming pool of the *Sonesta Beach Hotel*. In the pool, Burke teaches potential scuba divers the basics with mask, flippers, regulator, training tank, air, back-pack, harness, belt and weights and then takes them out off the south shore to depths of 10 to 25 feet. It's very safe because an instructor is present at all times. For more experienced divers, the depth can be up to 80 feet. Snorkeling cruises are also available as well as helmet diving and an escorted underwater walk.

Water Skiing

Another popular sport around the island is water skiing especially during the months from May to September. Water skiing is allowed in the protected waters of *Hamilton Harbour, The Great Sound, Castle Harbour, Mangrove Bay, Spanish Point, Ferry Reach, Ely's*

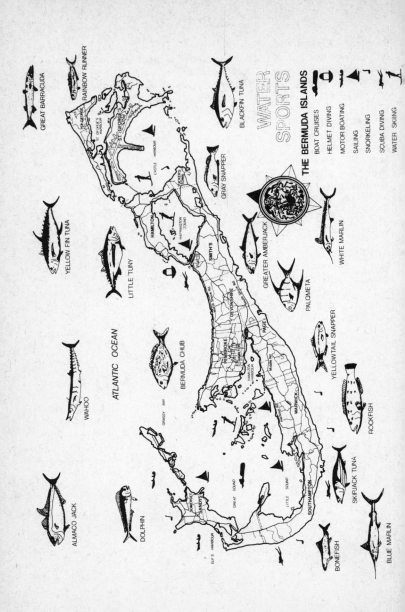

Harbour, Riddell's Bay and *Harrington Sound.* Bermuda law requires that water skiers be taken out only in boats operated by a licensed skipper, which are available at most hotel and cottage colony docks. Visitors who are not guests at these hotels may make arrangements with these, or other licensed operators on the island.

Windsurfing

Bermuda's windsurfing champion, Hugh Watlington, has recently opened a Windsurfing School at Glencoe, which will operate year-round, weather permitting. A 1½ hour lesson is approximately $25, board rental per hour is $12, and wet suits are available. All arrangements can be made directly with Hugh Watlington.

Horseback Riding

For those who want to get away from the water for a while, there is horseback riding at the *Warwick Riding School* on Middle Road, just across from Tamarind Vale Road. Here there are about 30 horses and ponies, two teaching rings, and conducted rides through the back hills and along sand dunes behind the south beaches.

Trail rides are about $12 per hour and there are breakfast rides on different days throughout the week. (Telephone 8-1822 for further information.) New in Devonshire is *Terceira's Stables* on Jubilee Road where two-hour beachcomber rides (6/6:30 A.M.) on Sundays and holidays cost $24 per person, including full breakfast. Daily trail rides on English or Western saddles are $12 per hour. (Telephone 2-7024 for further information.)

Squash

Players will not be disappointed since there are four squash courts on the island, located on Middle Road in Devonshire. The courts are available to visitors from 10 A.M. to 4 P.M. by reservation only, made by contacting the manager of the *Bermuda Squash Racquets Association*, Percy Foggo, at 2-6881, or write to the association, P.O. Box 176, Hamilton 5, Bermuda.

Bowling

Bowlers who can't stay away from the game, even on holiday, will want to know about *Warwick Lanes* on Middle Road in Warwick Parish. The lanes are open from 6 P.M. to midnight, Monday through Friday, from 2 P.M. to midnight on Saturday and Sunday. The charge is approximately $3.50 per game and shoes are available for a nominal fee. Bowling balls are free.

Fishing

Fishermen with visions of barracuda, dolphin, wahoo, rainbow runners, almaco jack and tuna will have some tall stories to tell about the great catch in the deep sea, off the reefs or shores of Bermuda. Fishing is a year-round sport in Bermuda but best from May through November, according to the local residents. The annual *Game Fishing Tournament* is in effect from May 1 through November and visitors are encouraged to enter their prize catch. The tournament, sponsored by the Fishing Information Bureau which is a division of the department of tourism, is for light or heavy tackle and 17 different species of game fish are eligible for awards when caught. Included among the most sought-after catches are Allison tuna, wahoo, great barracuda and greater amberjack. Awards of sterling silver fish pins are made for catches that meet or exceed stated weights for various methods of angling, casting, and general fishing. To win the pin, one must fill out a special form supplied by the fishing bureau and have it properly notarized. It takes a bit of an effort, but it is well worth it, participants say.

Bermuda offers three types of fishing—shore, reef or deep sea—all of which offer a variety of good catch. The most prized of all fish caught from the shore is the pugnacious bonefish and the best time is from early May to mid-July. Best locations for fishing are along *Whitney Bay* in Southampton, *Shelly Bay* in Hamilton Parish, the *Causeway and Castle Point* in St. George's. Other catch from the shore are likely to be: pompano, gray snapper, Jack, great barracuda (during the summer).

As the island is surrounded by some 200 miles of reefs, this type of fishing is a natural for those with some expertise and can look for yellowtail snapper, almaco jack, greater amberjack, gray snapper, porgy, redhind, little tunny and Bermuda chub.

Charter Boats

Skippered by experienced guides and accommodating from four to six persons, charter boats are available for deep-sea fishing with full day rates at $250 and half day at $150. They are equipped with fighting chairs and outriggers, all tackle, bait and other paraphernalia but visitors must bring their own lunch and refreshments. (No fishing license is required.) Varieties of the larger gamefish in Bermuda's offshore waters are tuna, marlin, dolphin, wahoo, greater amberjack, great barracuda, almaco jack, rainbow runner, skipjack tuna and little tunny (mackerel). (See chart for tackle and boat rentals.)

If you plan to have a real fishing holiday around the island, you might want your travel agent to make all the arrangements in advance but make your own payments in Bermuda because windy weather may hold you up for a day or two (and you will not be charged).

Sailing and Boat Racing

Bermudians are also natural sailors, following in the wake of their ancestors who earned their livelihood from the sea and built some fine boats from local cedar. Sailing and boat racing are probably the most popular sports on the island and the turquoise sea is chock full of small and large craft throughout the year. From January to November, the *Royal Bermuda Yacht Club* holds races every Saturday in a variety of classes including Solings, International One-Designs, Luders-16s, 5-0-5s and Lasers. In addition, the *Bermuda Offshore Cruising Association* holds races on the first Sunday of each month for ocean-going yachts. Smart, handmade, Bermuda-fitted dinghies raced about every other Sunday from spring through fall (beginning the end of May) in *St. George's Harbour, Hamilton Harbour,* and *Mangrove Bay* in Somerset. Visitors may also compete in sunfish races on *Harrington Sound* or in *Salt Kettle* in front of Reggie Cooper's Glencoe. Powerboat races are also plentiful and take place on Sunday from May to November at *Ferry Reach,* near the airport. There are both closed-circuit and offshore races and occasionally top drivers team up with locals to race.

But the real race is the almost 700-mile *Newport (Rhode Island) to Bermuda Yacht Race* that takes place in June on the even year (1982; 1984). This famous blue water classic has as many as 180 elegant entries, considered to be among the finest in the world's sailing yachts, which sail from Newport on a Friday in mid-June and arrive in Bermuda within three or four days. This is a most prestigious event and "race week" in Bermuda is as Derby Week in London or Grand Prix week in Monte Carlo. On the alternate odd years, there are other races but none so exciting as the Newport to Bermuda competition.

For visitors who just prefer the sea and the sun in a more leisurely way, there are several types of boats for rent by the hour or the day. Most of the large hotels have their own equipment for use of their guests and which may be available to other visitors upon request. Sail along with the wind and the waves, it's all a part of the wonderful sporting life in Bermuda!

*Sailing is a favorite island pastime. In addition to the New-
port-to-Bermuda race held every other year, there are nu-
merous small and large regattas for all to join.*

The nave of Bermuda's Anglican Cathedral on Church Street in Hamilton. Dedicated in 1894, its Gothic tower is a landmark for visitors arriving by sea.

The town of St. George, founded in 1612, was the colony's capital for over 200 years. Among its attractions are Ordnance Island, above, with a replica of the Deliverance, which was one of the two small ships built to take the shipwrecked passengers of the Sea Venture on to the Jamestown settlement. Below, the Stocks and Pillory in King's Square were once a place of punishment for the early settlers.

Gibbs Hill Lighthouse is visible to ships some 40 miles away. Visitors can climb its 185 steps for the finest view in Bermuda.

STAYING IN BERMUDA

From Hotels to Cottage Colonies

Whatever type of accommodations you choose in Bermuda, you will find them comfortable and pleasant and the service both friendly and efficient. The island's guest properties are of the highest quality, whether casual and informal housekeeping cottages or the sophisticated and luxurious resort hotels that are practically self-contained villages. Between these two categories, there is a choice of over 100 properties including the typically Bermudian cottage colonies and small guest houses that accommodate less than a dozen guests.

There are 11 large resort hotels with their own beach or beach club, pools, tennis and golf facilities. They also offer other resort amenities as nightclubs and entertainment, room service, social director who plans activities, shopping arcade, beauty salon and sauna, cycle livery, taxi stand, a choice of bars and restaurants. In public rooms in the evening, gentlemen are expected to wear jacket and tie.

The smaller hotels offer much the same service, with less activities and entertainment and there are no shops or beauty salon. Cottage colonies are uniquely Bermudian and feature a main clubhouse with dining room and bar, with private cottages spread around beautifully landscaped grounds. The cottage offers privacy while the clubhouse and other facilities (pool and tennis courts) offer the opportunity to mingle with the other guests. Some of the cottages have kitchenettes where a maid fixes breakfast every morning, and you can store your drink mixes (but cannot cook). All cottage colonies have a pool and some have the most glorious beaches in Bermuda.

There are both large and small housekeeping cottages and apartments throughout the island. These are much like cottage colonies but without a main clubhouse and the cottages or apartment-like units all have cooking facilities. The owners will guide you to the local supermarket which generally delivers and will give you a bill at the end of your stay. Some of the cottages have their own terrace and pool and the larger properties are situated along a beach front. These accommodations are excellent for families with small children, and babysitting can be easily arranged.

Most of the large guest houses are old Bermuda mansions that have been modernized to offer spacious bedrooms, dining room and lounge in the old house. Some have added other units in garden settings. The smaller guest houses are generally private homes that can accommodate less than 12 guests. The only meal offered is usually breakfast so you are free to try Bermuda's fine restaurants in the evening. Some of these guest houses are located on the water.

If you are planning to stay in Bermuda more than a month, it is possible to rent a private residence through a local real estate agent. Approximate prices range from $400 to $800 for a one-bedroom property; $1,500 to $2,000 for a two-bedroom home, and $2,000 to $3,000 for three bedrooms, per month. Maid service, food and utilities are extra. Write to the Bermuda Department of Tourism, 630 Fifth Ave., New York, N.Y. 10111 for a list of rental agents.

WHAT WILL IT COST? Bermuda has two seasons: A long summer or "high season" that lasts from about March 1 through November 30, and a winter or "low season" during the months of December, January, and February. Hotel rates differ greatly between these two seasons and you can find reductions of as much as 40 percent during the winter. There are, however, year-round packages at many of the island's properties that are excellent buys and bring your daily cost down considerably. There are golf specials as well as tennis, honeymoon, family, scuba diving (and any other name) packages that feature accommodations plus two meals daily, sightseeing tours, transfers to and from the airport, complimentary tennis or golf, etc.

Prices quoted for Bermuda hotels and cottage colonies are MAP (Modified American Plan) and feature breakfast and dinner daily. In some instances, exchange dining can be arranged between hotels with the same ownership (Princess and Trusthouse) and other properties may give their guests a chit to dine outside but you must pay transportation and the overage charges. Prices quoted in brochures do not include 5 percent Bermuda tax or service charges. The island-wide service charge is between 10 and 15 percent but many properties add a straight $4.50 per person, per day to your bill to handle this, plus a $2 to $4 fuel surcharge to pay for oil. Many *Bermuda Hotels now accept credit cards for payment.* If they do not, your bill must be paid in cash, travelers' checks or by a personal check (pre-arranged with the management).

Large Resort Hotels: Prices vary among them, but you can expect to pay from $70 to $125 MAP per person (double occupancy) per day in high season. Low season 1981/82 rates from December 1 to March are about 10% less, for MAP.

Small Resort Hotels: The 12 small hotels range in price from $50 to $80 per person (double occupancy) per day in high season. Low season 1981/82 rates are somewhat less from December 1 to March. The plan is MAP.

Cottage Colonies: There are 7 cottage colonies, all with main clubhouse and cottages spread around lovely grounds. The rates range from $50 to $100 per person (double occupancy) per day in high season. The plan is generally MAP.

Clubs: There are two private clubs in the luxury category and require introduction by a member. They are the Coral Beach and Tennis Club, and the Mid Ocean Club. Prices on request.

Housekeeping Cottages and Apartments (large): These are efficiency units with separate cottages or apartments. Of the 20 listed, the average rates range from $30 (no meals) and from $60 (MAP). Bermuda Plan (breakfast only) is also available from $37 per person (double occupancy). Low season rates are about 40 percent less.

Housekeeping Cottages and Apartments (small): There are 15 of these properties. The rates are very low, from about $25 per person (double occupancy) with no meals or $30 with full Bermuda breakfast (BP). Most of these properties have a swimming pool or waterfront, or are near a public beach. None has evening entertainment. Prices are less in winter, although many are closed.

Guest Houses: There are now about 40 guest houses on the island ranging from large to very small (less than 12 guests). Prices and plan also vary from MAP ($30 per person) to EP (no meals) for less than $20 per person per day. Some also offer BP (Bermuda breakfast) or CP (Continental breakfast) plans. Prices are much lower in winter. As these places have no sports facilities, they will appeal to those who are not interested in the outdoor life Bermuda has to offer, or those on a tight budget.

It is best to describe the many properties in Bermuda in the classifications the hotel association has given them, i.e. type and size. All of the properties can be described as ''top class'' although some are more luxurious and more expensive than others. And readers must forgive the occasional oohs and aahs that appear in these descriptions, for although the food can occasionally disappoint, the settings of some of these places are unparalleled and the owners deserve several stars for the imaginative use of the landscape.

EDITORS' CHOICES'

On our third stay at **Elbow Beach Hotel** recently, we found this 30-acre resort its usual beehive of activity. New cottages were being completed, the *Seahorse Surf Club* built, and down on the famous Elbow Beach about 1,000 college kids gathered for a traditional Monday-morning party.

Through it all, Elbow's manager Austin Mott III walked unfazed, greeting the guests, supervising the construction, meeting with his staff. The remarkable aspect of Elbow Beach Hotel is that several activities can be taking place at the same time but none of it need bother you. Besides the lovely beach, there are superb tennis courts, and the resort is only about ten minutes' moped ride from the center of Hamilton. It's hard to believe that in 1908 this was a small guest house known as the South Shore Hotel.

Bermuda is known for its ''Cottage Colonies,'' and **Cambridge Beaches** is the original. On 25 acres between the Atlantic Ocean and Mangrove Bay, this cottage colony is the epitome of the best Bermuda has to offer. The main house is built around a 17th-century cedar-beamed lodge, and a lower terrace is made of old grindstones recovered by neighbor Teddy Tucker, a well-known diver, from the English brig *Caesar,* which foundered on the reefs in 1818. Good neighbor that he is, Teddy Tucker even laid the stones.

Cambridge Beaches has 33 Bermudian cottages scattered around its lovely property, plus "Pegem," a 300-year-old cottage that has now been restored for guest occupancy. Pegem has English antique furniture and a full kitchen and dining room. Cambridge Beaches will provide a cook/maid for guests who wish it. Otherwise, there is dining in the main house and dancing on the edge of Mangrove Bay.

Reggie Cooper's **Glencoe** is a small hotel with subtle style. It is the pride of Salt Kettle. Reggie is a sailor, and all his friends drop by on weekends to discuss their boats and the latest in maritime gossip. If you like, Reggie will lend you a Sunfish, or you can just sit on the terrace and watch the fun. Glencoe has a charming ambience and interesting guests. It is a delightfully small, high-quality place that is convenient to Hamilton as well as outside sports facilities.

LARGE RESORT HOTELS

Belmont Hotel & Golf Club, Warwick Parish. Situated atop 110 acres overlooking Hamilton Harbour and across the Great Sound, this well-established resort hotel does not seem as though it accommodates between 300 and 400 guests who can play golf out the sidedoor, tennis a few steps down from the terrace or swim in a vast, heated salt pool. A steep climb down to the ferry dock and you can catch the boat to Hamilton, a picturesque 15 minutes away ($1). The hotel offers complimentary transportation to its South Shore beach club (shared with the Bermudiana and Harmony Hall hotels). All three properties are managed by the English company, Trusthouse Forte and exchange dining among the triumvirate is available. A bevy of activities are arranged each week by the social hostess and there is entertainment nightly in one of the lounges. All three hotels sell an "Insider's Passport" worth about $75 in tours and fun around the island. Deluxe rooms at the Belmont overlook the harbor; moderate ones view the green hillside. There are good packages available. *(MAP;BP)*

Bermudiana Hotel, Pembroke Parish (downtown Hamilton). Smack in the middle of town, this large pink structure overlooks Hamilton Harbour and accommodates approximately 500 guests. In its spacious gardens are a large heated pool as well as an indoor pool, and two tennis courts. Guests have privileges at the Belmont golf course as well as the South Shore beach club. Front

Street shops and the ferry dock are just around the corner, and there is dancing nightly in the *Du Barry Room* and *Hoop-a-Loo Discotheque*. A la carte lunch and dinner are available in *La Fontaine Restaurant* daily. A middle-class hotel in the middle of town that doesn't make you feel you're surrounded by a small city. Good packages are available. *(MAP;BP)*

Castle Harbour Hotel, Tucker's Town. A world unto itself on 250 acres, this hotel was built for the passengers of the Furness-Withy Steamship Line in the early '30s. Old-age splendor impresses the minute you walk in the door, large public rooms with original beams, a cavernous cellar full of shops and bars, two large pools (one with its own gentle current), a lovely outdoor garden/terrace with bar and perfect for summer barbecues, plus a complete country club. The 18-hole Castle Harbour golf course is one of the best on the island, and a new wing was added in 1968 to accommodate golfers. The rooms are spacious, with lovely views, even if it takes a good 15 minutes to get to them from the front lobby. This is the largest privately owned property in Bermuda (650 guests) and there are six all-weather tennis courts, a Yacht Club and Marina besides everything else. Try the two private beaches when you are tired of the two swimming pools. Several restaurants including the *Windsor Dining Room, Golf Club Tavern, Café Cascade and Pool Terrace*, and a snack area for busy athletes in the golf wing. Different shows every evening and dancing nightly in the *Knight Club*. Afterward, take a stroll on the grounds—the moon looks bigger and brighter from here. Castle Harbour is about a $8 taxi ride from Hamilton, but just

RESORT HOTELS

LARGE HOTELS

1 BELMONT HOTEL
2 BERMUDIANA HOTEL
3 CASTLE HARBOUR HOTEL
4 ELBOW BEACH HOTEL
5 GROTTO BAY BEACH HOTEL
6 HOLIDAY INN
7 INVERURIE HOTEL
8 PRINCESS HOTEL
9 SONESTA BEACH HOTEL
10 SOUTHAMPTON PRINCESS HOTEL

SMALL HOTELS

11 CORAL ISLAND HOTEL

12 GLENCOE
13 HARMONY HALL HOTEL
14 NEWSTEAD
15 PALMETTO BAY HOTEL AND COTTAGES
16 POMPANO BEACH CLUB
17 REEFS BEACH CLUB
18 ROSEDON
19 HAMILTONIAN HOTEL
20 WATERLOO HOUSE
21 WHITE SANDS AND COTTAGES
22 MERMAID BEACH CLUB
23 STONINGTON BEACH HOTEL

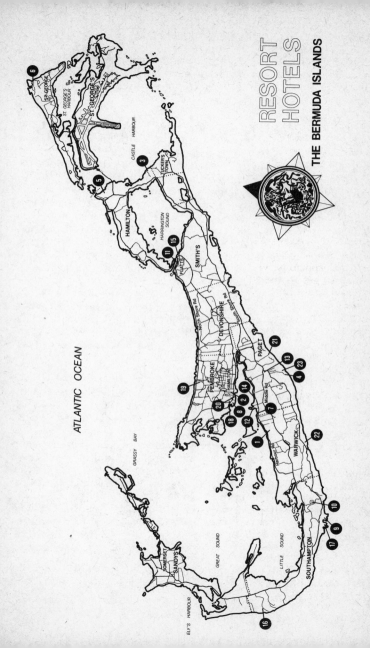

RESORT
HOTELS
THE BERMUDA ISLANDS

ATLANTIC OCEAN

ST. GEORGE'S

ST. GEORGE'S HARBOUR

CASTLE HARBOUR

TUCKER'S TOWN

HARRINGTON SOUND

HAMILTON

FLATTS

SMITH'S

North Shore Rd

South Shore Rd

DEVONSHIRE

PEMBROKE

PAGET

Middle Rd

Harbour Rd

WARWICK

GRASSY BAY

GREAT SOUND

LITTLE SOUND

SOUTHAMPTON

SOMERSET

SANDYS

ELY'S HARBOUR

across from the airport (you can both hear and see the landings) in one of the high-rent districts. The hotel has undergone recently the first stage of an extensive renovation project. Golf, tennis and honeymoon packages. *(MAP)*

Elbow Beach Hotel, Paget. Until recently known as the Elbow Beach Surf Club, this property along the South Shore began as a small guest house in 1908. The main house is situated on the crest of a hill that sweeps down to a glorious beach, complete with *Seahorse Surf Club* and deluxe surf-side lanais that overlook it. The 550-plus guests are accommodated in the main house as well as private cottages and lanais that dot the 30-acre property, much like a cottage colony. The property is beautifully landscaped and if you don't like to walk up and down the hills, a mini-bus travels the service road to pick you up. This is a swinging place with five tennis courts, plenty of water sports and nightly entertainment in the *Peacock Room* and new *Seahorse Pub,* one of the nicest new spots on the island. An "in" place always, especially for the college crowd during the spring. The resort is in a constant state of rejuvenation, improving the old and adding on the new. In fact, a total of 36 junior suite/cottages has been added and fit in beautifully. Elbow Beach is a place where you can do a lot or a little but always in luxurious surroundings. Honeymoon, tennis and family packages available. *(MAP)*

Grotto Bay Beach Hotel and Tennis Club, Hamilton Parish. One of the smallest of the large resort hotels, Grotto Bay is a series of modern townhouse-type structures laid out along the ocean's edge. All nine "lodges" have private balconies overlooking the sea. The property encompasses 20 acres and features lots of tennis and water sports. There are two underground "grottos" and one has been turned into a fun discotheque called *Prospero's Cave*. The other can be inspected (on bended knee) during the day. The main house is modern and well-appointed and a large swimming pool is just a hop from a small beach. Bermuda's newest hotel is perfect for the honeymoon crowd. Tennis, family, vacation and honeymoon packages are available. *(MAP;BP)*

Holiday Inn, St. George's. Overlooking the town of St. George on one side and Fort St. Catherine on the other, this large hotel

(600-plus guests) has a 9-hole golf course, 4 tennis courts, and a beautiful private beach. Lots of action in a very Holiday-ish Inn way. Two lobbies, two swimming pools, nightclub, and full social staff. It's a nice-looking building on the outside (Bermuda pink) but too air-conditioned and dark on the inside—not quite Bermudian enough. Only large, luxury hotel in St. George's Parish. *(MAP)*

Inverurie Hotel, Paget Parish. A resort hotel on the water's edge, overlooking Hamilton Harbour, that has grown in recent years from small to fairly large with the addition of new buildings across the road. It sits beside Darrell's Wharf where the Hamilton ferry stops for the ten-minute ride to town. The club offers free transportation to two south shore beaches daily, a Roman bath pool on the upper level with harbor view, cycle livery and taxi stand on premises, and imported entertainment as well as dancing in *La Cabaret Nightclub* or outdoor on *Marine Terrace.* Pleasant harbor views from *Salt Kettle Lounge* and *Marine Bar.* Sailing, water-skiing and deep-water swimming from the Marine Terrace, two tennis courts free for guests and the Belmont Golf Club just a few minutes' walk up the road. Inverurie is a good first-class hotel but definitely not in the luxury category. *(MAP)*

Princess Hotel, Hamilton. Named after Princess Louise, the daughter of Queen Victoria, who came to the island for the winter of 1883, this was the colony's first and foremost hotel for many decades. The site has been considerably rebuilt since the 19th century and, although the property is attractive and luxurious, it does not have that sense of history one might expect. However, the Princess is in the pink and a hotel that offers convenience to town (5 minutes walk), lovely views of the harbor, and all the sports privileges of the Southampton Princess. Complimentary shuttle buses between the two hotels carry guests for golf, swimming, tennis, and exchange dining. The Hamilton Princess has all the amenities of a large hotel (shopping arcade, beauty shops, etc.) and two swimming pools on the water's edge. Fishing, sailing and water sports can be arranged from its own private dock. Guests may dine in the *Three Crowns* or *Tiara Room* restaurants or get meal credits for the *Whaler Inn, Waterlot Inn,* etc., in Southampton. There is entertainment nightly in the *Princess Lounge* as well as dancing in the *Gazebo Bar.* This is a large hotel (over 900 guests) that feels large. It's good for groups and offers three- and four-night packages. *(MAP; Gourmet Plan)*

Sonesta Beach Hotel, Southampton. Another large luxury resort hotel right on the water, Sonesta handles its recent 606 guests well. The majority of the rooms overlook the sea or Sonesta's own cove; the others look up Gibbs Hill. A $6 million renovation program included 60 new deluxe rooms and suites. There are six all-weather lighted tennis courts, free of charge to guests, good fishing from the Sonesta shore, scuba diving and instructor at the edge of the cove, two large pools (one covered with a glass dome), social director and lots of action. Well-managed hotel with good food in the *Port Royal* dining room, local entertainment and dancing in *Fiddler's Green*. Beautifully landscaped 25 acres of grounds, with children's playground, underwater observation lounge, and 18-hole putting green. Convenient to three golf courses. Good hotel for families, groups and couples. Offers honeymoon, tennis, and scuba special packages. Expensive but worth it! *(MAP)*

Southampton Princess, Southampton. The other Princess hotel on the island, this one sits atop a 60-acre estate with a commanding view of all Bermuda. Over 1,000 guests flock to this large, self-contained resort and love its international atmosphere. In fact, you could be anywhere in the world in this hotel—it's that kind of place. Why leave the premises? There are two shopping arcades, beauty salons, health club, two swimming pools, a private beach club with *Whaler Inn* and *Shipwreck Bar,* 11 tennis courts, fishing and other water sports, and 18-hole executive par-3 golf course, several restaurants as well as the *Waterlot Inn* down on the other shore, and top-rate entertainment in the *Empire Room,* disco dancing in *Half and Half,* and a combo in *Neptune Bar* and *Shipwreck Bar* nightly. Why leave, indeed? There is even a new Lobby Bar with casual dress code. This resort hotel has everything in a flashy sort of way. If you get a bit tired of it all, you can always take a complimentary bus into the Hamilton Princess to get another view. There are even 100 suites, including a deluxe suite that has 3 double bedrooms, living room, 4 baths, and a balcony from which the view is magnificent, if you're not afraid of heights. Rates are expensive but honeymoon, tennis, golf packages are available. *(MAP)*

SMALL HOTELS

Coral Island Hotel, Hamilton Parish. Close to delightful Flatt's Village, the Coral Island Hotel has a main house that looks like a country inn. Situated on Flatts Inlet, this small hotel has grown to over 170 guests, including four cottage units at the nearby Breaker's

Club. There are water sports from the hotel dock or the Breakers Club beach, and exchange facilities with Palmetto Bay, a short walk around the inlet. The hotel is under new management and has been completely refurbished, with very elegant suites. A 25-year plan for time-shares is being phased into the hotel, although it will continue to take guests now. *(MAP;BP;EP)*

Glencoe, Paget. Located in Salt Kettle and almost completely surrounded by water, this cozy small hotel has a following of friendly guests who return over and over to enjoy the ambience of this historic Bermuda home. A one-minute walk from the ferry dock (Salt Kettle), there is swimming in the garden pool, a small sandy cove for swimming, sailing and water skiing. Tennis and golf can be arranged up the road at Belmont. Sunfish free to guests, and a year-round Windsurfing School has just been opened by Bermuda's Windsurfing champion, Hugh Watlington. Charming place for about 70 guests. *(MAP;BP)*

Hamiltonian Hotel and Island Club, Pembroke Parish. Lovely views from atop Mt. Langton above Hamilton, this small hotel can accommodate 134 guests on 3 floors. It has a large pool and 3 all-weather tennis courts with pro and teaching aids. Dining room known for panoramic views and lobster in season. Convenient to town, which is just down the hill. *(MAP;BP)*

Harmony Hall, Paget Parish. The smaller sister of Belmont and Bermudiana, Harmony Hall is surrounded by beautifully landscaped lawns and gardens. The 144 guests stay in cottage-type rooms in the main building or in units around the garden. There is a small pool and complimentary transportation is provided daily to the South Shore Beach Club. There are two tennis courts, a putting green, and shuffleboard on the grounds. Golf can be arranged at Belmont and exchange dining at both Belmont and Bermudiana where the evening's entertainment can also be found. "Insider's Passport" also sold here. This is the best of both worlds—friendly and small but offers guests the use of the facilities at the two larger properties. Honeymoon, golf and passport special packages. *(MAP)*

Mermaid Beach Club, Warwick Parish. Housekeeping apartments and hotels for 150 guests right on the ocean, along the south shore. Restaurant on premises and meals available at *Miramar.* Pool plus private beach. Informal and lively bar with entertainment during the season. Modern one- and two-bedroom apartments, suites and bed/sitting rooms with private balconies and fully equipped kitchens on request. *(MAP;BP)*

Newstead, Paget Parish. Another beautiful old Bermuda manor house that has sprawled out along the edge of Hamilton Harbour. It's as pretty from the water as it is in the well-groomed grounds and gardens. Flowers bloom year-round as you walk into the main house with its panoramic view of Hamilton across the way, and it's a two-minute walk down to the ferry dock. This is one of the favored places on the island, with its own special charm and coziness. Large, heated pool and saunas, barbecues on the terrace in the evening. Although Newstead can accommodate over 100 guests, it's still like staying in a private home. Golf, tennis and beach club can be arranged by the management. Superb value for the money. *(MAP;BP)*

Palmetto Bay Hotel and Cottages, Smith's Parish. Modern guest rooms and cottage units for 84 persons are located on the edge of Harrington Sound and Flatt's Village. The main house is another old Bermuda mansion with a comfortable lounge, *Ha'Penny Pub,* dining room and terrace overlooking the pool and sound. Good boating and swimming from the dock, tennis, golf and other water sports can be arranged by the management. Guests can use Breakers Beach club nearby. Golf, health/beauty, and honeymooner special packages are offered. *(MAP;BP;EP)*

Pompano Beach Club, Southampton Parish. Cottage units for 86 guests are dramatically placed on a hillside overlooking the ocean. Every room with a view! Dining in the main clubhouse overlooking the ocean. Pool and bar on the upper level; down below, a small beach and private dock. Boat for reef fishing and scuba diving leaves from here. There is one clay tennis court for guests and golf can be arranged at nearby Port Royal Golf Course. Informal, casual atmosphere here that has great appeal. Honeymoon, golf and family special packages. *(MAP;BP)*

The Reefs Beach Club, Southampton Parish. A casually elegant cabana colony perched on a cliff overlooking the south shore and its own private beach. There is room here for over 100 guests but it seems much smaller and more intimate. The large, secluded beach has snack and bar facilities and there are two new all-weather tennis courts. If they're crowded, walk along the shore to Sonesta Beach. Informal dancing in the evening but not much entertainment. However, Sonesta and Southampton Princess are just up the road. David Dodwell is now owner as well as manager. Book far ahead. Honeymoon, golf and tennis packages are offered. *(MAP;BP)*

Rosedon, Pembroke Parish. Colonial charm in the main house of this small hotel (64 guests) in Hamilton, across the road from the Princess Hotel. Accommodations include breakfast only in your room, on the veranda or by the pool. It's a five-minute walk into town when you can tear yourself away from the lovely grounds. Exchange tennis at Elbow Beach Hotel and other sports can be arranged. Rosedon is the perfect spot for a quiet, do-it-yourself holiday. *(BP)*

Stonington Beach Hotel, Paget Parish. A brand new $7.4 million hotel and school run by the Bermuda Department of Hotel Technology. Located on 22 beautiful acres of the Stonington Estate (right next to Elbow Beach Hotel), it has accommodations for about 128 people in cottages overlooking the sea. Guests are taken care of by students at the hotel school. Pool. Two tennis courts. Excellent manager and reputation. *(BP;MAP)*

Waterloo House, Pembroke Parish. Conveniently located in Hamilton, this small harborside hotel can accommodate 70 guests who are given keys to the large cedar door at street entrance when they go out in the evening. A short walk to Hamilton and the ferry. Garden pool and other sports facilities can be arranged. Honeymoon Special package. *(MAP;BP)*

White Sands and Cottages, Paget Parish. Overlooking Grape Bay on the south shore, this small hotel (80 guests) has an informal and casual atmosphere and is just the place for families and honeymooners who do not want organized activity. Cottages are below the main house and Grape Bay Beach is a six-minute walk. Lovely views from outdoor terrace overlooking the sea where weekly swizzle parties and barbecues take place. Special monthly rental for some cottages. *(MAP;BP;EP)*

COTTAGE COLONIES

Ariel Sands Beach Club, Devonshire Parish. Lovely location along the south shore, and groups of cottages situated up and down low-grade hill. There are 11 cottage units in all with private porch. Three all-weather tennis courts plus a large swimming pool with patio and snack bar. Reef-snorkeling equipment is available for rent, but *beware* of the reefs. A pleasant and restful place for some 90 guests. One of the guests likes the place so much, she donated a wire statue that plays in the foaming surf. Perfect for couples or families. Informal dancing outdoors, barbecues and candlelight buffets. Very personable management. *(MAP;BP)*

Cambridge Beaches, Sandys Parish. Some say this is the nicest cottage colony of all. It is the original, dating from 1922. A total of 132 guests live in lovely cottages around a 25-acre estate on Mangrove Bay. Main house has a section that is about three centuries old. The whole area is entirely surrounded by water with beautiful beaches on all sides—five to choose. Outdoor terrace overlooking the bay and private dock for fishing and touring boats. It's a 15-minute walk to Watford Bridge for ferry to Hamilton, just a few minutes by cycle into Somerset, a little longer out to the Maritime Museum. Water sports feature skiing, sailing, pedalos and deep sea fishing. There are three all-weather tennis courts and golf can be arranged elsewhere. *Port O'Call Bar* and *Residents Bar,* plus dancing twice weekly. Look at the impressive list of repeat guests engraved on wooden plaques. It's a secluded and heavenly place for all ages. *(MAP)*

Flamingo Beach Club and Cottages, Warwick and Southampton parishes. This is a recent amalgamation of the Flamingo Beach Club and Montgomery Cottages with a total capacity for 22 guests. All cottages (except 10 units at Flamingo Beach) have fully equipped kitchens. At Flamingo Beach, cottage units are in a garden setting overlooking the south shore and ocean. The whole is a relaxed atmosphere with a variety of accommodations to suit all tastes in a central location. *(EP)*

Horizons and Cottages, Paget Parish. Another impressive old Bermuda mansion around which cottages have been set in a hillside garden. This is our favorite choice of a cottage colony in a central location (across from Elbow Beach and catty-corner from Coral

COTTAGE COLONIES AND CLUBS

1 ARIEL SANDS BEACH CLUB	6 PINK BEACH CLUB
2 CAMBRIDGE BEACHES	7 WILLOWBANK
3 FLAMINGO BEACH CLUB	8 CORAL BEACH AND TENNIS
4 HORIZONS & COTTAGES	CLUB
5 LANTANA COLONY CLUB	9 MID OCEAN CLUB

COTTAGE
COLONIES
& CLUBS
THE BERMUDA ISLANDS

ATLANTIC OCEAN

ST. GEORGE

ST. GEORGE'S HARBOUR

ST. GEORGE'S

CASTLE HARBOUR

HAMILTON

HARRINGTON SOUND

TUCKER'S TOWN

SMITH'S

FLATTS

North Shore Rd

South Shore Rd

DEVONSHIRE

PAGET

PEMBROKE

HAMILTON

HAMILTON HARBOUR

Middle Rd

WARWICK

Harbour Rd

GRASSY BAY

SOMERSET

SANDY'S

GREAT SOUND

LITTLE SOUND

SOUTHAMPTON

ELY'S HARBOUR

Beach and Tennis Club). Located along the South Shore Road and overlooking Coral Beach, which guests may use, the cottages climb quite a hill here up to the main house. There are 3 all-weather tennis courts, a 9-hole mashie golf course and 18-hole putting green on the property, as well as a large pool and sun terrace. Dinner is served in or out-of-doors, depending upon the weather and nightlife is accessible at the large hotels in the area. It's an informal and friendly place that has a host of aficionados. *(MAP;BP)*

Lantana Colony Club, Sandys Parish. The most elegant of all the cottage colonies, this choice property overlooks the Great Sound from Sandys Parish. The clubhouse is pure Bermudian and the 100-plus guests live in luxurious cottages around the area. All have private porches, kitchenettes for cold breakfast-in-bed, and are equipped with hair dryers and irons. There are two all-weather courts, putting green, croquet lawn, shuffle-board, private dock for water skiing and sunfish, plus large pool and *La Plages* restaurant for lunch and drinks. The ferry ride to Hamilton from Somerset Bridge (30 to 45 minutes) is complimentary to guests. But who wants to leave? The *Meridian Lounge* and *Carousel Bar* are elegant and the *Solarium* dining room is like dining in a greenhouse. It's famous for the poinsettias at Christmastime. Lantana is closed for six weeks beginning the second week in January. *(MAP)*

Pink Beach Club, Smith's Parish. A quiet colony of pink cottages surrounding a private beach along the south shore, this property can accommodate 128 guests. There are 20 acres of landscaped grounds, a main clubhouse, large pool and terrace, two all-weather tennis courts, dancing and barbecues for the guests. High rates for an exclusive, quiet area. *(MAP)*

Willowbank, Sandys Parish. A simple cottage colony located on Ely's Harbor on the south shore with religious overtones. Morning devotional period is set aside for those who wish to attend. Meals are served family-style in the main dining room. No liquor is served. Accommodations for 114 guests in cottages on seven acres of grounds. There is a swimming pool and one tennis court. Ideal for a quiet family vacation. *(MAP)*

CLUBS

Coral Beach and Tennis Club, Paget. This is a private club and introduction by a member or former guest is required. There are accommodations for 133 guests on a lovely beach property along the south shore. Excellent tennis facilities on 7 courts, with a tennis pro and Round Robin tournaments on Sunday. There are 2 squash courts, an 18-hole putting green, lawn bowling and croquet on the premises. Beautiful beach. Guests and members may use the swimming pool and 9-hole mashie golf course at Horizons & Cottages across the road. Dinner is served in main clubhouse (formal on Thursday and Saturday nights). Informal *Beach Terrace* with bar overlooking the large, private stretch of beach. *(MAP;BP;EP)*

Mid Ocean Club, Tucker's Town. Introduction by a member is definitely required at this distinguished Bermuda club in fashionable Tucker's Town. A large estate on the edge of the ocean that has played host to statesmen from Britain, France, and the U.S., it has its own private 18-hole championship course plus two all-weather tennis courts. Rates only on request for 32 guests.

HOUSEKEEPING COTTAGES AND APARTMENTS (LARGE)

Arlington Heights, Smith's Parish. Four minutes from Flatts Village, these modern apartment and cottage units can accommodate 44 guests in a garden setting. Lovely pool and own private beach nearby. All have kitchenette and some have balcony. *(EP)*

Astwood Cove, Warwick Parish. Modern, bright apartments for 24 guests on South Shore Road, close to public beaches. *(EP)*

Banana Beach Ocean Front Apartments, Warwick Parish. Housekeeping apartments for 54 guests overlooking the ocean or pool. Private beach and guest lounge overlooking ocean. Groceries can be delivered at no extra charge. *(EP)*

Belljori, Warwick Parish. Guest capacity is now 26 in housekeeping apartments on Warwickshire Estate, off South Shore Road. Large pool and within walking distance of Warwick Long Bay. *(EP)*

Blue Horizons, Warwick Parish. Comfortable apartment units for 23 guests with a large pool, lawn and terrace, and lounge in the main house. Supermarket nearby and close to south shore beaches, hotels, entertainment. *(EP)*

Clairfront Apartments, Warwick Parish. Housekeeping units for 16 guests plus one bedroom in the main house in the residential area of Warwickshire Estate, off South Shore Road. Private swimming pool and sun deck and close to south shore beaches. *(EP)*

Clear View Apartments, Hamilton Parish. Formerly known as the Gay View Apts., these units for 20 are located on the water's edge off North Shore Road. Fishing, swimming and snorkeling off own waterfront. Near Flatt's Village for shopping and entertainment. *(EP)*

Longtail Cliffs, Warwick Parish. Modern housekeeping apartments for 48 guests overlooking the ocean. All have covered porches, and there is a private beach. Swimming pool and maid service. *(EP)*

Marley Beach Cottages, Warwick Parish. You may recognize this lovely location along the south shore from the popular film *The Deep.* Housekeeping units for 46 guests, with pool and lovely beach below. Continental breakfast served on pool terrace if desired. Good location and pleasant management. *(CP;EP;MAP)*

Mermaid West Apartments, Warwick Parish. Efficiency units ideal for families, close to all south shore beaches and near restaurants. Casual, informal. Private pool and guest capacity for 32. *(EP)*

HOUSEKEEPING COTTAGES & APARTMENTS

1 ARLINGTON HEIGHTS
2 BANANA BEACH OCEAN FRONT APARTMENTS
3 SANDPIPER
4 LONGTAIL CLIFFS
5 MARLEY BEACH COTTAGES
6 GARDEN HOUSE
7 MERMAID WEST APARTMENTS
8 MUNRO BEACH COTTAGES
9 ROSEMONT
10 SOMERSET BRIDGE APARTMENTS
11 SOUTH CAPERS
12 SURF SIDE BEACH CLUB
13 BELLJORI
14 BLUE HORIZONS
15 BY FAITH APARTMENTS
16 CABANA VACATION APARTMENTS
17 CAPTAIN WILLIAMS BAY
18 CLAIRFONT APARTMENTS
19 CLEAR VIEW APARTMENTS
20 GLENMAR HOLIDAY APARTMENTS
21 GRAPE BAY COTTAGES
22 HONEY HILL
23 HARRINGAY APARTMENTS
24 ASTWOOD COVE
25 MIDDLETON COTTAGES
26 PARAQUET GUEST APARTMENTS
27 SANDON COTTAGES
28 SKY TOP
29 THALIA
30 SUN TAN APARTMENTS
31 SYL-DEN APARTMENTS
32 PRETTY PENNY
33 VALLEY COTTAGES
34 WATERVILLE VACATION APARTMENTS
35 PILLAR VILLE

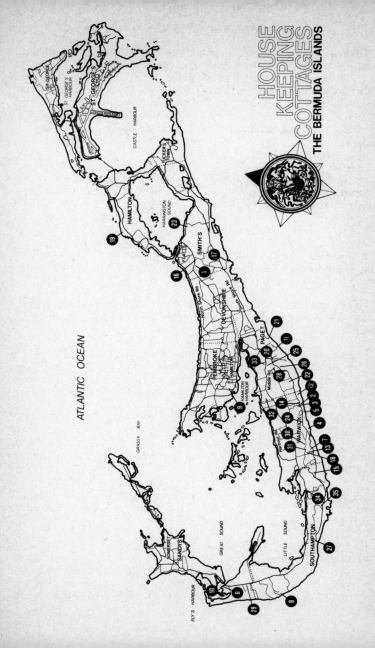

HOUSE
KEEPING
COTTAGES
THE BERMUDA ISLANDS

ATLANTIC OCEAN

Munro Beach Cottages, Southampton Parish. Attractive, modern duplex cottage units less than 100 yards (91 meters) from the beach on Whitney Bay, along the south shore. Bordered on three sides by Port Royal Golf Course, with its own extensive grounds. Guest capacity is 32 in secluded area. Excellent for families. *(EP)*

Paraquet Guest Apartments, Paget. Large, modern bedrooms with veranda for 20 guests in residential district on South Shore Road, with restaurant on premises. *(EP)*

Rosemont, Pembroke Parish. Housekeeping units for 56 guests situated on a hillside overlooking Hamilton Harbour. Just a short walk to town and ferry. Apartments are built on two levels, with penthouse deck and large pool. Children's play area and laundry facilities. Wheel chair guests welcome. *(EP)*

Sandpiper Guest Apartments, Warwick Parish. Modern and spacious apartments with 6 efficiency units on South Road. Close to beaches. *(EP)*

Sky Top, Paget. Informal guest house for 18 persons in residential area. Double bedrooms and apartment units, some with kitchenette. *(EP)*

Somerset Bridge Apartments, Sandys Parish. Overlooking Ely's Harbour and just a short walk to the Somerset Bridge ferry, these self-contained apartments can accommodate 26 guests. A small beach cove and private dock below with good swimming. *(BP;EP)*

South Capers Cottages, Paget. Self-contained modern apartments and cottages accommodate 46 guests and overlook the ocean on the south shore. There are 2 private pools and it's a three-minute walk to Grape Bay Beach. Perfect for families with children (laundry facilities). *(EP)*

Sun Tan Apartments, Warwick Parish. Modern efficiency apartments for 18 guests in central residential area of Lusher Hill, Spice Hill Road. Entertainment nearby. *(EP)*

Surf Side Beach Club, Warwick Parish. A varied group of cottages and apartments overlook the south shore from landscaped, terraced levels. Beautiful pool (one for children too) as well as a private beach. Large sun terrace and coffee shop open from 8:30 A.M. to 3 P.M. Accommodation for 74 guests in lovely location. *(EP)*

Waterville Vacation Apartments, Southampton Parish. House-keeping units for 22 guests overlooking Great Sound, located opposite Waterlot Inn on Middle Rd. Close to restaruants and entertainment. *(EP)*

HOUSEKEEPING COTTAGES AND APARTMENTS (SMALL)

By Faith Apartments, Southampton Parish. Efficiency units for 10 guests, some with porch, convenient to Horseshoe Bay. Casual and informal accommodations in residential area. Close to south shore facilities. *(EP)*

Cabana Vacation Apartments, Smith's Parish. A two-centuries-old Bermuda house redesigned into comfortable, self-contained apartments, each with private entrance. Cedar-beamed clubroom, large pool in garden setting. Accommodations for 16 guests in informal and friendly atmosphere. Located on Verdmont Road. *(EP)*

Captain William's Bay, Smith's Parish. The main house is a modern Bermuda home with large living room, spacious lawn terrace and pool. Three bedrooms in main house plus two apartment units with kitchen. Guest capacity is 10 and property is situated on the water's edge in residential area. *(EP;CP)*

Garden House, Sandys Parish. Located just at Somerset Bridge and managed by Rosie Galloway, Garden House accommodates 12 persons in cottages for two or four. *(BP;EP)*

Glenmar Holiday Apartments, Paget. Efficiency apartments for 12 guests in residential area on St. Michel's Road. Comfortable lounge. Upper apartment has open porch, lower apartments open onto lawn. Centrally located. *(EP)*

Grape Bay Cottages, Paget. Various-sized cottages in secluded settings that can accommodate 20 guests. Good locations in three different areas, convenient to south shore beaches. *(EP)*

Harringay Cottages, Smith's Parish. An old manor house with cottages in landscaped hillside garden overlooking Harrington Sound. Swimming from own sand terrace and dock. Informal, friendly atmosphere and convenient to Flatt's Village. Guest capacity is 10. *(BP;EP)*

Honey Hill Apartments, Paget. Licensed last year, there are five housekeeping apartments on the South Road. Convenient to beaches. *(EP)*

Middleton Cottages, Paget. An old Bermuda house, off Middle Road, converted into self-contained apartments for 17 guests with spacious grounds and informal atmosphere. *(EP)*

Pillar-Ville, Southampton Parish. Housekeeping cottages for 16 persons, with panoramic views over south shore and ocean. Convenient to beaches. *(EP)*

Pretty Penny, Paget. Bright, comfortable accommodations for 12 guests on Cobb's Hill Rd. Small pool and patio in secluded garden. Charming antiques in main house. *(CP;EP)*

Sandon Cottages, Southampton Parish. Cottage units for 6 guests in a hillside garden estate with sweeping views of the sea. Swimming just across the road at Church Bay. Close to other beaches, golf, and horseback riding. *(EP)*

Syl-Den Apartments, Warwick Parish. Housekeeping apartments for 10 guests close to south shore beaches. Informal atmosphere in residential area of Warwickshire Estate, off South Road. *(EP)*

Thalia, Sandys Parish. Units for 18 guests on hill overlooking Port Royal Golf Course and a five-minute walk to beach cove. Old Bermuda home with informal atmosphere. *(BP)*

Valley Cottages, Paget. Informal old Bermuda cottages and self-contained apartments for 23 guests opening onto garden setting. Near Elbow Beach and supermarket. *(EP)*

GUEST HOUSES (LARGE)

Archlyn Villa, Pembroke Parish. Informal accommodations for 30 guests overlooking Mill's Creek and Fairylands. Large lounge and solarium, spacious garden. *(CP;EP)*

Buena Vista, Paget. Informal guest house with secluded garden overlooking Hamilton Harbour. Small private beach and boating on the harbor. Close to ferry and bus and excellent for families. Accommodations for 43 guests. *(MAP;BP)*

Loughlands, Paget. A stately old Bermuda mansion with accommodations for 43 guests. Extensive grounds and gardens. Family-style lounge and dining room. Convenient to beaches, golf and entertainment. *(BP)*

Royal Palms, Pembroke Parish. Accommodations for 20 in spacious gardens. Quiet and hospitable. *(CP)*

Sugar Cane Hotel, Sandys Parish. Situated in a relaxed garden setting in Somerset, this informal place takes 26 guests. Pool in small garden plus private sandy cove on Great Sound. Near two public beaches and village of Somerset. Tennis and golf nearby. *(MAP;BP)*

White Heron Country Inn. Old Bermuda mansion converted into guest accommodations for 20. Located on a small inlet in Riddell's Bay. Run-down by our standards. Noisy pub and working-class atmosphere. Two platform tennis courts and swimming pool. Three golf courses and beaches nearby. Double rooms plus apartment suites. *(MAP;BP)*

Woodbourne/Inverness, Pembroke Parish. Three guest houses with total accommodation of 28. Within walking distance of Hamilton and ferry. Comfortable and informal. *(CP)*

GUEST HOUSES (SMALL)

Ashley Hall, Devonshire. Accommodations for 14 on South Shore Road, some overlooking pool. Spacious garden and convenient to Hamilton. *(CP)*

Bayridge, Pembroke Parish. Accommodations for 10 on Woodbourne Avenue with lounge and dining room. Walking distance to Hamilton and ferry. *(BP)*

Burch's Guest House, Devonshire. A Bermuda home with bedrooms for 12 guests overlooking north shore. Small garden. *(EP;BP)*

Canada Villa, Pembroke Parish. Informal accommodations for 12 guests. Large swimming pool and terrace, within walking distance of Hamilton. *(EP)*

Edgehill Manor, Pembroke Parish. Outskirts of Hamilton, with accommodations for 18. Pool and patio in garden area. *(CP)*

Fariesville, Paget. An old Bermuda home with large bedrooms for 12 guests, large garden, and patio with pool. Informal and convenient. *(BP)*

Fordham Hall, Pembroke Parish. Rooms for 22 guests with large lounge downstairs, sitting room with harbor view upstairs. *(CP)*

The Gables, Paget. Interesting old Bermuda home for 10 guests, a one-minute walk from Hodgson's ferry dock. Large, airy bedrooms and close to Hamilton for shopping. *(CP)*

Granaway Guest House, Warwick Parish. A 300-year-old mansion on Harbour Road with panoramic views of the Great Sound. Private dock for deep-water swimming; delightful garden. Accommodations for 10 in large bedrooms. Informal atmosphere and close to ferry. *(CP)*

Greenbank and Cottages, Paget. Old Bermuda house and cottages in Salt Kettle, one minute from ferry dock. Family-style living and dining areas, outdoor patios and verandas. Accommodations for 18 guests. *(CP;EP)*

Hillcrest Guest House, St. George's. Old Bermuda home with large veranda and views of St. George's Harbour. In historic area. Accommodations for 17 guests. Large garden and spacious lawns. *(BP;CP)*

GUEST HOUSES

1 ARCHLYN VILLA	15 HILLCREST
2 BUENA VISTA	16 THE GABLES
3 LOUGHLANDS	17 LITTLE POMANDER
4 HI-ROY	18 MAZARINE BY THE SEA
5 SUGAR CANE HOTEL	19 OXFORD HOUSE
6 WOODBOURNE INVERNESS	20 PLEASANT VIEW
7 ASHLEY HALL	21 ROYAL HEIGHTS
8 BAYRIDGE	22 SALT KETTLE HOUSE
9 BURCH'S GUEST HOUSE	23 SEVEN ARCHES
10 CANADA VILLA	24 ROYAL PALMS
11 EDGEHILL MANOR	25 GRANAWAY HOUSE
12 FARIESVILLE	26 TALLENT VILLA
13 FORDHAM HALL	27 WHITE HERON
14 GREENBANK AND COTTAGES	

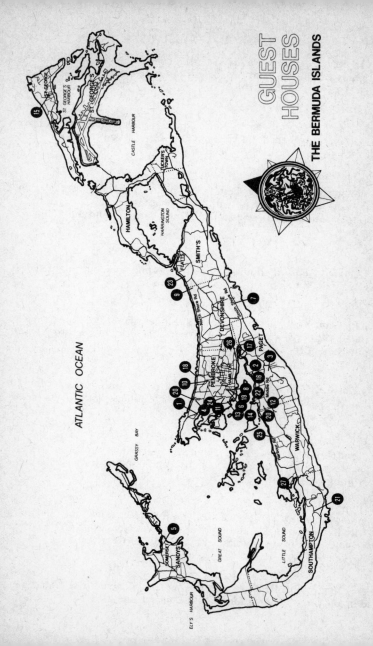

GUEST HOUSES

THE BERMUDA ISLANDS

Hi-Roy, Pembroke Parish. Small, modern guest house in Princess Estates off North Shore Road. Large Lounge, home-cooked meals for 11 guests. *(MAP;BP;EP)*

Little Pomander, Paget. Located on edge of Hamilton Harbour. Casual atmosphere for 10 guests. Old Bermuda cottage with waterfront garden patio and barbecue. *(CP)*

Mazarine By The Sea, Pembroke Parish. Located on water's edge on north shore. Pool and patio with panoramic view of ocean. Accommodations for 14 guests in modern bedrooms and self-contained units. *(EP)*

Oxford House, Pembroke Parish. Informal and comfortable guest house for 20 persons near Hamilton and ferry. *(CP)*

Pleasant View, Pembroke Parish. Modern guest house in Princess Estate off north shore road for 10 persons. Ocean views from patio. Convenient to Hamilton. *(BP;EP)*

Royal Heights, Southampton. Bedrooms with terraces for 10 guests. Swimming pool and comfortable lounge with views of the Great Sound. Informal accommodations on Lighthouse Hill. *(BP)*

Salt Kettle House, Paget. Rooms, cottages and apartments for 14 guests in garden setting. Small cove and dock on harbor inlet with swimming. *(BP)*

Seven Arches, Smith's Parish. Old Bermuda home on large estate with lovely gardens and rooms for 9 guests. Near Flatt's Village and private dock for swimming and snorkeling. *(CP;EP)*

Tallent Villa, Pembroke Parish. Guest house with secluded garden and large veranda for 9 guests. Near Hamilton. *(BP)*

SMALL HOUSES (less than 12 beds)

Belleterre, Pembroke Parish. Informal guest house for 6 guests in residential area in Spanish Point. Panoramic views overlooking Mill's Creek. *(BP)*

Glenn Folly, Paget. Quiet guest house on St. Michael's Road with large bedrooms and small garden. Accommodates 6 guests. *(CP;EP)*

Kennington, Devonshire Parish. Small guest house with pleasant garden and quiet surroundings. Accommodations for 6 guests. *(BP)*

Kimbar Terraces, Pembroke Parish. Small guest house in garden setting in Cavendish Heights. Walking distance to Hamilton. 6 guests. *(BP)*

Que Sera, Paget. Small guest house for 6 (1 housekeeping apartment) near Botanical Gardens. Close to Hamilton and south shore. *(EP)*

Seaward, Paget. Informal guest house with kitchen facilities in Salt Kettle. Private dock and pool. Near ferry. 10 guests. *(EP)*

Sound View Cottage, Southampton Parish. Housekeeping units for 6 guests. *(EP)*

Southsea, Paget. Stately old house on hilltop overlooking Botanical Gardens. Large bedrooms for 8 guests and large lounges. Close to Hamilton and beaches. *(CP)*

South View Guest Apartments, Warwick Parish. Three housekeeping units for 6 guests. Located in Khyber Pass. *(EP)*

Stu-Kay, Pembroke Parish. Guest house and housekeeping units for 8 guests. *(BP;EP)*

Tree Tops, Paget Parish. An old Bermudian home divided into three efficiency units with a large veranda. Located in the residential area of Cobb's Hill Road. Five minutes' walk to the bus stop, ten-minute ride to beaches. Casual and informal. *(EP)*

Wainwright, St. George's Parish. Small, informal guest house near town of St. George. Accommodations for 8 guests. *(BP)*

SMALL GUEST HOUSES (Less than 12 beds)

1	BELLETERRE	7	KIMBAR TERRACES
2	SOUTH VIEW	8	WAINWRIGHT
3	TREE TOPS	9	SOUND VIEW COTTAGE
4	GLENN FOLLY	10	STU-KAY
5	QUE SERA	11	SOUTHSEA
6	KENNINGTON	12	SEAWARD

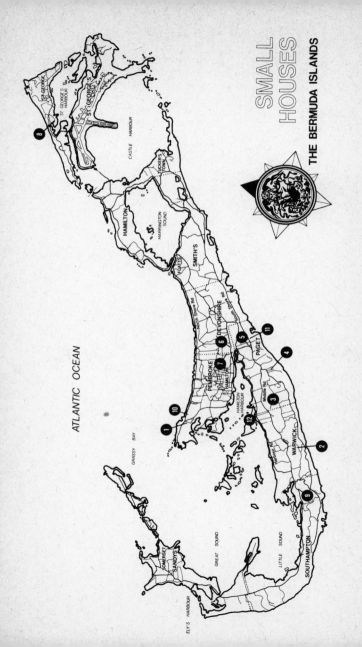

DINING, WINING AND ENTERTAINMENT

By Candlelight or Alfresco

The end of a perfect day in Bermuda means dining on a lovely terrace under a twinkling sky, or indoors with candlelight bouncing across century-old cedar beams. It also means a short motorbike ride to a popular spot to try the local specialties. The island is full of restaurants that serve traditional Bermudian dishes, English and Continental, gourmet fare that is equal to any in the world, or finger food like hamburgers and french fries that taste extra good in the salt air. The choice is all yours—and you may want to try them all!

Traditional Bermudian fare features the many varieties of fish found in the surrounding sea, plus local fruits and vegetables. Many of the recipes have been handed down among families for generations. Indeed, the favorite Christmastime dish of cassava pie is said to be a 300-year-old tradition. It is a meat pie with the dough flavored by the cassava root and no good Bermudian home is without its appearance right next to the very-English plum pudding at holiday time. Another time-honored island custom is Sunday breakfast when the menu is salt cod and bananas. This fruit is one of the local staples and Bermudians bake them, fry them, fritter them as well as use them in puddings and bread. The sweet Bermuda onion is another local favorite and popular dishes are onion pie, cheese and onion sandwiches, and even glazed in sugar and rum for dessert!

Fish, the major source of nourishment for the early colonists, is creatively used in a number of local specialties. The most famous, of course, is fish chowder which is served laced with as much black rum and sherry peppers as you like. (Sherry peppers are simply made by marinating hot, spicy peppers in sherry for several weeks. Replenish sherry as you use and let "mull" some more.) Restaurant menus also feature red snapper (with onions and potatoes), mussel pie, mussel fritters, Bermuda shark, and succulent Bermuda spiny lobster (in season from mid-September through March). Hoppin' John and Bermuda syllabub are two other dishes that should not be overlooked. The former is a mixture of rice, peas, onions, bacon, thyme and chicken and served as a main course. The latter is a dessert that combines guava jelly, wine and cream. Delicious!

If you wish to dine at the more elegant and expensive restaurants on the island, it is best to book ahead and check on the dress requirements. Many restaurants, especially in hotels, request that gentlemen wear a jacket and tie and that their companions are also appropriately garbed. Dinner prices in these restaurants compare to those in other resorts and can run up to $50 per person, depending upon the number of courses chosen and types of drinks and wine. Expect a 15 percent service charge on top of everything you and your companion consume.

Many of the larger restaurants (with the exception of those in hotels and cottage colonies) will accept credit cards, mainly *American Express,* but *Master Card* and *Visa* are also accepted at a few. If you do not wish to pay cash, check credit information when you call to book a table.

ELEGANT AND EXPENSIVE

Fourways Inn, Paget. At the very top of fine dining in Bermuda, this gourmet restaurant is in an 18th-century Georgian home full of highly polished cedar beams and balustrades. It is a culinary adventure and, indeed, your meal will be remembered long after you have paid the bill. The menu is impressive and specialties include fresh mussels simmered in white wine and cream, fresh veal sautéed in lemon butter, Caesar salad and strawberry soufflé for dessert. But every dish here is a specialty and served with a flourish. Carafe wine available as well as excellent wine list, all drinks; the Fourways Special combines loquat liqueur with juices and bitters. Open

DINING, WINING AND ENTERTAINMENT 153

seven days a week for lunch and dinner (brunch now served daily, with Gourmet brunch on Sundays) and dining is outside in season. An irresistible pastry shop is open on the premises Mon.–Sat. (Reservations: 2-6517)

Henry VIII Pub-Restaurant, Southampton Parish. Equally top-rate but a more relaxed atmosphere in Tudor surroundings with service by charming young ladies dressed as "wenches." Wooden tables and chairs and diamond-paned windows that open up in the summer. The restaurant is located at the top of the hill, overlooking Sonesta Beach Hotel and the south shore. Very popular with the local residents. Local Bermudian and English fare features beef, juicy lamb, mussel pie, steak and kidney pie, and seafood casseroles. Wonderful onion soup, turtle soup, and hearty King and Queen salads. Elizabethan evenings once a week with troubadors to entertain. Lots of fun! Lunch and dinner plus Sunday brunch. Gourmet shop attached. (Reservations: 8-1977; 8-0908)

Newport Room, Southampton Princess. An elegant gourmet restaurant on the first floor of the Southampton Princess Hotel with décor of a yacht's dining room, exquisite china and Waterford crystal. The most intimate and romantic place on the island. The continental menu is extensive and features both European and Bermudian specialties with an American clientele in mind. Fresh Bermuda grouper and rockfish, scampi, chicken American, lamb, veal and beef are all included. There is a new emphasis on *nouvelle cuisine* that makes everything taste fresher and more succulent than ever. The seafood and fish are wonderful—scampi with mushrooms or Dover sole with scallops and shrimp. Delicious steamed fresh vegetables and crisp cold salads. Lemon ice cleanses the palate between courses. Excellent wine list, but trust the suggestion of the wine steward. For dessert, there are crepes flambees (flaming pancakes with vanilla ice cream), bananas flambees (Bermuda bananas flamed with dark rum), cherries jubilee with kirsch, souffle of the day and a trolley of cakes and pastries. The Newport Room is open daily, for dinner only, from 7 P.M. (Reservations: 8-8000)

Papillon, Church and Burnaby Streets, town of Hamilton. This chic dining spot is presided over by four European chefs who prepare an extensive Continental menu daily. House specialties include Rockfish sautéed with almonds and bananas, red bean soup, cream of mussel soup, Medallion of steak with morel sauce, and a fantastic Surprise Dessert. Elegant, expensive and romantic (with lovely dance floor). (Reservations: 5-0333)

Tom Moore's Tavern, Hamilton Parish. One of the most pleasant places on the island for a meal or just a rest stop on the motorbike.

Sit on the veranda and relax in the surroundings of an historic home where Irish poet Tom Moore came to call during his sojourn on the island in 1804. The house was actually built in 1652 and was a private home until about 75 years ago when it was turned into a tavern. The walls are full of quotations and the calabash tree Moore immortalized in his verse still exists in the backyard. If it's a warm day have a Tom Moore Special, made with the local loquat liqueur and several juices, and sit under the famous tree. The menu favors local fish but one can also have steaks, duckling or Cornish game hen stuffed with wild rice. Specialty of the house is fish a la Moore, which is broiled and then topped with a cream sherry sauce and chopped mushrooms (delicious!). Fresh lobster in season (Sept. 1 to March 31) is also available. As the dining rooms are small and ceilings are low, try to pick a table that is not surrounded by large parties of people or you will not be able to hear your companion speak. Dining here is a lovely experience both for the food and the atmosphere. Open daily for lunch from 12 noon and dinner from 7 P.M. (Reservations: 3-1166; 3-0090)

Waterlot Inn, Southampton. Located on a sheltered cove just below Gibbs Hill Lighthouse, this site by the water's edge has been an inn for 300 years. The present structure is new but has an historic feeling (it was rebuilt three years ago following a fire). Waterlot is a gourmet restaurant, on a par with the best, with dining outdoors on the terrace in summer and a private pier for guests who arrive via boat for lunch or Sunday brunch. Dinners are candlelit and romantic. Specialties include Bermuda rockfish, broiled scampi, le Bermuda Triangle (lobster tail, steak and veal), l'entrecote au poivre Toulouse-Lautrec (pepper steak flamed at the table), coq au vin, veal and beef dishes. Desserts include homemade ice cream, crepes, cherries jubilee and baked Alaska flamed with brandy as well as the memorable la coupe Fosco (homemade raspberry and orange sherbert with fresh strawberries and sherry melba sauce). Open daily for dinner from 7 P.M. and lunch from 12 noon. Sunday, brunch only from 12 noon. (Reservations: 8-0510)

EXCLUSIVE SPECIALTY RESTAURANTS

Approximately $15 to $30 per person

Carriage House, St. George's. Filling a need for a top-rate restaurant in the middle of St. George's, the Carriage House is in the new Somers Wharf Plaza, in an old storehouse that adjoins the Carriage Museum. The brick arches have been maintained to give the restaurant an airy, old-world look. The atmosphere is more casual than elegant, but the food is fine. The menu features roast beef, steaks and chops, with two giant salad bars and homemade bread. Tap beer from the bar as you enter, plus drinks and wine. Try for a window and a view of St. George's Harbour. Enter from the plaza and browse around afterward; it's very well done. Open for lunch from 11:30 and dinner from 6:30. Families with children welcome. (Reservations: 7-1730)

Crown and Anchor, St. George's. Located in the newest part of Somers' Wharf area in historic St. George, this charming pub-cum-restaurant overlooks the water, of course, and offers a clean, wholesome atmosphere for both the traveler and the local. Great for both lunch or dinner. Luncheon menu served from 11:45 A.M. to 2:45 P.M. daily and features seafood, fish and chips, steak and jumbo shrimp. Dinner from 6:30 to 10:45 P.M. Seafood, chicken or steaks served by 6-, 10- or 14-ounce portions and charged accordingly. Good salads and soups. Folk music from 7-11 P.M. Closed Sundays. (Reservations: 7-1515)

Ding Ho, town of Hamilton. Oriental restaurant in the Belvedere Building on Pitts Bay Road that offers a cross between Chinese cuisine and that of the South Pacific. Begin in the Tiki Lounge with a Scorpion, Suffering Bastard or Samoan fog cutter and a plate of Pupu (appetizer). Move on to the Orient or Lotus rooms for Kun Bo Gai Din, Gai Kew Steak, etc. (Don't worry, it's all delicious so come hungry.) Special lunch and dinner menu and outgoing orders. Dinner only on weekends. (Reservations: 5-2167)

Fisherman's Reef, town of Hamilton. Located above the popular Hog Penny Pub on Burnaby Hill in the center of Hamilton, this seafood restaurant specializes in local fare and traditional Bermudian dishes. Lobster in season is the chef's pride, but all fish here is good. Under same management as the Lobster Pot and full a la carte menu. Casual dress allowed. Open daily except Sunday for lunch from 12 noon and dinner from 6:30 P.M. (Reservations: 2-2534)

Harbourfront, town of Hamilton. Situated right on Front Street, opposite the Ferry Terminal and Visitors Bureau, the décor is nautical and view from the small terrace is that of a bustling harbor. Choices are the terrace, Binnacle Bar and Captain's Table. A casual place with fair food, best for lunchtime snacks but dinner menu features fish chowder, steaks and roast beef, fresh Bermuda fish and lobster, and Crepes Suzette. Open Monday through Saturday from 11 A.M. Bar open until 1 A.M. (Reservations: 5-4207)

Little Venice, town of Hamilton. Now one of a few Italian restaurants on the island, Little Venice is located on Bermudiana Road. Pasta, scampi and veal are served in a pseudo-Mediterranean atmosphere with wine in the carafe or by the bottle. Service can be very snide if you're only a visitor and not a regular. Upstairs, The Club discotheque opens at 10 P.M. (Reservations: 5-3503)

Lobster Pot, town of Hamilton. Reputed to be the best seafood restaurant on the island. Located on Bermudiana Road with a fisherman's cove atmosphere. Specialties are fresh oysters year-round, Bermuda fish of all types, lobster pot pourri (seafood in a curry sauce), or steak and lobster tail combination. Bermuda lobster in season; Maine lobster the rest of the year. Lunch and dinner daily (except Sunday) from 11:30 A.M. to 5 P.M. and 6 P.M. to 11 P.M. (Reservations: 2-6898)

Penthouse Club, town of Hamilton. Right on Front Street, upstairs from the Longtail Bar, this is an old favorite among the local residents and among the nicer restaurants on the island. Continental menu in a classy décor. Both Bermuda fish and beef are featured in a variety of haute cuisine methods, while appetizers and desserts are strictly gourmet. End the meal with Crepes au Grand Marnier and enjoy the flames! Ask for the window overlooking the harbor. Lunch (Monday through Friday) from 12 noon; and dinner (Monday through Saturday) from 7 P.M. (Reservations: 2-3414)

Plantation, Hamilton Parish. Adjoining Leamington Caves, this restaurant is strictly Bermudian fare and features homemade fish chowder, Bermuda lobster in season, steaks, veal and chicken. The Plantation Salad features avocado, mushrooms, onions and croutons. Desserts are from the Plantation Sweet Trolley. Watch Out! Wine list, drinks and Irish Coffee.

Rum Runners, town of Hamilton. Formerly the Hoppin' John, this restaurant on Front Street has a new nautical decor and boasts two patios (one overlooking Hamilton Harbour), three indoor dining rooms and two pub-style bars. A la carte dining in the main room in the evening (jacket and tie required) but casual during the day and in the other areas at night. Menu is American, English and European with Bermuda lobster in season and fresh seafood a specialty. Lunch and dinner. (Reservations: 2-4737)

The Waterfront, town of Hamilton. Right on the waterside on the edge of Hamilton Harbour down where the private boats are buoyed. Very Bermudian and popular with the local residents. Specialties of the house are Bermuda fish of all sorts, lobster in season and seafood, plus stuffed pork chops, chicken curry, veal with wine sauce, and frogs legs provençale. Open daily for lunch and dinner but closed Saturday lunch and all day Sunday. (Reservations: 1-3181)

Whaler Inn, Southampton Princess. Right on the beach overlooking the south shore, this beach club restaurant offers fine food and a pleasant atmosphere. Lunch is casual and hectic because of all the sunworshippers at the beach club, but dinner is pleasant and relaxed. Specialties include flaming pirate's sword for 2 (beef on a skewer with vegetables), captain's favourite dish (pot pourri of chicken, scampi, fish and beef) as well as other meat and fish entrees. All dinners include a trip to the salad table. The desserts are not unusual, but there is an extensive wine list. Open daily for lunch from 12 noon and dinner from 7 P.M. Dancing nightly on the terrace. Sunday brunch from 12 noon. (Reservations: 8-0076)

MEDIUM-PRICED RESTAURANTS

($6 to $12 for lunch; $10 to $20 for dinner)

Black Horse Tavern, St. David's Island. A friendly, local restaurant with no pretentions. Fresh fish and seafood are the specialty of the house, especially shrimp, scallops, curried mussels, lobster in season, fish chowder and shark. Open daily for lunch and dinner; carry-out service. (Reservations: 7-1999; 7-1079)

Botanic Garden, town of Hamilton. Located in Trimingham's, this is a favored spot for a shopping stop. Lunch and tea served from 11:30 A.M. to 3 P.M. Open sandwiches, homemade soups, cakes, pastries, yogurt and fruit salads. Managed by Fourways Inn, so you know it's first-rate. Many different types of tea, coffee and mineral water to drink.

Il Chianti (formerly Camden Tavern), Paget. Situated on the grounds of the Botanical Gardens, this Italian restaurant is hung with Chianti bottles from the ceiling, has bright tablecloths and an Italian menu. Candlelit in the evenings. Open daily (except Sunday) for lunch (11:30 to 2:30 P.M.) and dinner (7 to 11 P.M.). (Reservations: 1-6056 or 1-6360)

Ye Olde Cock and Feather, town of Hamilton. A Bermudian pub in the middle of Front Street, serving British and Scottish brew. Hearty food like steak and kidney pie, shepherds pie, fish and chips, sausage and mash, and hamburgers. Open daily (except Sunday) and lunch served from 11 A.M. to 6 P.M. Happy hour from 5:15 P.M. to 6:15 P.M. (Telephone: 5-2263)

Dennis's Hideaway, St. David's Island. Owner Dennis Lambe serves up hard-to-find dishes in this quaint eating place that is accessible by land or sea on St. David's Island. Specialties are conch fritters, shark hash, turtle steaks, seafood stews and chowders. Hamburgers and hotdogs are also on hand for the less imaginative palates. No bar, but Mr. Lambe will chill your wine. (Reservations: 7-0044)

Hog Penny Pub, town of Hamilton. Informal dining at reasonable prices halfway up Burnaby Hill, opposite the flagpole on Front Street. English-pub atmosphere with English draft beer and ale, fish and chips as well as local fish and seafood. Other dishes available. Open daily from 11 A.M. to 1 A.M., Sundays from 6 P.M. to 1 A.M. Casual dress and lively entertainment nightly. (Reservations: 2-2534)

Horse and Buggy, town of Hamilton. This is a Tudor-style pub/ restaurant on Queen Street (near Church Street), with an informal atmosphere that offers a varied menu for lunch and dinner. Good for lunchtime snack, or a friendly dinner when the pub's entertainers lead a sing-along. Very modest establishment but you get to mingle with the locals in a candlelight atmosphere. Smart casual dress is acceptable. (Reservations: 2-6699)

The Ice Cream Parlour, Hamilton Parish. Just catty-corner from the Swizzle Inn, this is a great place to go for dessert. Homemade ice cream and open daily from 11 A.M. to 7 P.M. Parking available and cute tables outside on the patio so you can rest between sight-seeing or mopeding. Hotdogs, coffee, tea and hot chocolate also available but stick to the cones, milkshakes, sodas, banana and pineapple boats. Yummy!

Longtail Restaurant, town of Hamilton. Named after Bermuda's national bird, this restaurant is located on the foot of Burnaby Hill, next to the Hog Penny. Two floors: the lower for quick snacks while shopping; the upper offers the diner everything from Hungarian goulash to Wiener schnitzel to fresh Bermuda fish. Sit out on the terrace and "people watch." Casual attire for a casual place. (Reservations: 2-3414)

Loyalty Inn, Sandys Parish. Another unpretentious place, this one in a 250-year-old Bermuda home just 5 minutes' walk from the Watford Bridge ferry landing. Caters to visitors and locals in the Somerset area for luncheon snacks, afternoon drinks and dinner. Seafood is the backbone of the a la carte menu. (Reservations: 4-0125)

Paraquet, Paget. Casual restaurant and snack bar on South Shore Road near entrance to Elbow Beach Hotel. Fresh vegetables, soups (fish chowder, Portuguese bean soup) are filling for lunch, but also open for breakfast and dinner seven days from 9:30 A.M. to 1:30 A.M. (good for midnight snacks). No cocktail lounge. (Reservations: 1-6060)

Pedro's (formerly the Breakers Club), Smith's Parish. A beautiful setting for what is now a tacky taco place. Fast foods a la Mexico. Eat in, dine out, self-service. Open from 11 A.M. to 10 P.M. (March 1 to Dec. 24) and 5 P.M. to 10 P.M. (Jan. 2 to Feb. 28). Bar service available. (Telephone: 3-1811)

Port Royal Golf Course, Southampton Parish. This handsome restaurant overlooks the sea and the 18th hole of the championship Robert Trent Jones-designed government golf course. Visitors most welcome for steak sandwiches and English beer after the game but complete meals are also served. Open for breakfast from 8:30 A.M., lunch from 11 A.M. to 3 P.M., and snacks until dusk. Dress is very casual (but no spikes, please). (Reservations: 4-0236)

Portofino, town of Hamilton. Located on Bermudiana Road a few yards from Front St., Portofino specializes in pizza and pasta. It offers 13 different varieties of pizzas or Portofino's special lasagne and canneloni. Licensed for wine and beer and drinks. Dress is casual but smart. Open daily 11:30 A.M. to 1 A.M.

Pub on the Square, St. George's. Smack on King's Square in the middle of historic St. George's town, this British-type pub offers cool draft beer after a morning of sightseeing, and juicy hamburgers or fish and chips. Reasonable. (Reservations: 7-1522)

Ram's Head Inn, town of Hamilton. Comfortable pub located on Pitts Bay Road (near Bermudiana Hotel). Quick lunches are a specialty among decorations of mounted ram's heads, bright blue tartan carpet and seat coverings. Darts, games room, beer on tap. This Scottish-type pub is open from 10 A.M. to 1 A.M. and serves dinner as well as sing-along entertainment nightly. Visitors are welcome to "stop in for a pint" after a heavy day. (Reservations: 5-0567)

Robin Hood, town of Hamilton. Choice of hearty fare in surroundings that try to emulate the Blue Boar pub of Sherwood Forest days. Lunch is hot and cold buffet called "Friar's Tuck-in" and served with a "foaming ferkin" (a measure of ale). Table d'hôte menu in the evenings and entertainment in Tuck's Room. Three bars. The restaurant is located on Richmond Road. (Reservations: 5-3314)

San Giorgio Ristorante, Water Street, St. George's. Rustic, reasonable and very new. Italian cuisine and pastas featured. A good selection of pizzas may be ordered for take out. Open for lunch and dinner daily except Sunday. (Reservations: 7-1307)

Somerset Country Squire, Sandys Parish. Bermudian and English dishes are a specialty at this country inn overlooking Mangrove Bay in Somerset. Charming and restful atmosphere after a long day on the motorbike. Have a rum swizzle in the sun on the terrace. The best Bermuda lobsters on the island when in season. (Reservations: 4-0105)

Swizzle Inn, Hamilton Parish. Even the name is marvelous—and home of the famous Rum Swizzle that has successfully found its way around the entire island. Located just west of the airport, near the Bermuda Perfume Factory and cave area, this is a popular place to stop while touring. Sit outside in good weather and watch the other motorbikes whiz by. Have a swizzle and a game of darts while you wait for your "swizzleburger" to come. (Reserv.: 3-0091)

Town and Country, town of Hamilton. Located on the corner of King and Reid Streets, Arthur Monkman's restaurant is an unpretentious eatery that offers heaps of home-cooked Bermudian dishes. The sandwich menu at lunchtime is impressive, and the dinner selections lean heavily toward fresh Bermuda fish, with rockfish, lobster in season and fisherman's platter the specialties of the house. (Reservations: 2-5680)

La Trattoria, Washington Lane, city of Hamilton. Catty-corner and down the lane from City Hall, this distinctive Italian restaurant is good for a simple lunch or dinner. Open daily from 10 A.M. to 11 P.M. for pastas, pizzas and other Italian specialities, there is also a good take-out service.

White Horse Tavern, St. George's. Facing King's Square and the harbor, this old tavern with a wide veranda is located on the edge of the bridge to Ordnance Island. Local and very simple food but sit on the veranda and give the fish your bread crusts. (Reserv.: 7-1838)

MODERATELY PRICED RESTAURANTS AND COFFEE SHOPS
(No bar unless specified)

($2.50 to $5 for sandwich and soft drink)

City of Hamilton: Arcade, Blue Moon, Buckaroo, Café Glace, Dorothy's Coffee Shop, Mannies, Spot Restaurant, The Coffee Cup Cafe, The Barnacle, Hamilton Pharmacy, Earl of Sandwich, Kentucky Fried Chicken, Continental Gourmet, The Bus Stop, Wheels Restaurant, Food Hut, Portofino Pizza.

St. George's Parish: Regatta Restaurant (airport), Tavern on the Green.

Hamilton Parish: Half Way House (with bar).

Pembroke Parish: The Green Lantern.

Southampton Parish: Horseshoe Bay Snack Bar, Riddell's Bay Restaurant, Wagon Wheel.

Sandys Parish: Hitching Post, Sunburst Restaurant.

In addition to the many restaurants already mentioned, all of the large hotels, some of the small and the cottage colonies, welcome visitors for dinner and their evening entertainment. If you are not in accommodations where breakfast and dinner are part of your plan, it is fun to hotel-hop. In fact, it's a good way to educate yourself on what the other properties have to offer. They all have a style of their own, and you will enjoy getting to know them. It is essential to call ahead as they may be fully booked (especially during popular long weekends) and be sure to check on dress requirements. As a general rule, gentlemen are expected to appear in jacket and tie and ladies will feel most comfortable in long skirts (take a wrap for air conditioning). These restaurants are fairly expensive and you should be prepared to pay in cash or travelers' checks as credit cards are not honored in hotel or cottage colony restaurants. Dinner hours also vary as many properties have two sittings. During the summer

months, many of these properties also offer an outdoor barbecue
that is popular, with dancing under the stars and some sort of local
entertainment. It is a set menu and price, plus service charge and
what you drink.

CITY OF HAMILTON, PEMBROKE PARISH

The Bermudiana Hotel. Located near the middle of town, this
hotel has the *La Fontaine* restaurant, with a real live fountain in the
middle. Casual during the day but with candlelight in the evenings.
Open from 6 P.M. to 10 P.M. daily except Thursdays. Weekly barbecues on the terrace it overlooks. Food only fair. Begin your evening
with a drink in the *Hamilton Bay,* lovely view of the harbor. (Reservations: 5-1211)

Hamilton Princess Hotel. This stately pink hotel on the harbor has
several restaurants of which *The Tiara Room* is the most posh and
definitely fit for a princess. Elegant in the evening and carefully
selected dishes cooked to perfection. *Le Bistro* has a more informal
atmosphere that tends to reflect Mediterranean cooking. Casual
during the day and convenient for the pool crowd. Watering holes
include the *Colony Bar, Gazebo Bar* and *Princess Lounge*. (Reservations: 5-3000)

Hamiltonian Hotel. High atop Langton Hill, the *Hamiltonian
Dining Room* is famous for local lobster in season, Maine lobster at
other times. Panoramic view of the city and harbor and Mr. Sherwood will personally greet you. Informal outdoor barbecues in summer on the terrace. (Reservations: 5-5608)

Waterloo House. This little harborside hotel on the edge of Hamilton has a small, friendly and very Bermudian dining room. The hotel
is associated with Coral Beach, Horizons and Newstead. (Reservations: 5-4480)

ST. GEORGE'S PARISH

The Holiday Inn. There are several eating places in this very-
American hotel overlooking St. George's Harbor and the main chan-

nel; on the other side is Fort St. Catherine. Call and inquire what the action is. There always is some. Begin in the *Sea Venture* bar or *Mid-Atlantic* cocktail lounge and move onward and upward. Highly air conditioned so dress accordingly. (Reservations: 7-8222)

HAMILTON PARISH

The Coral Island Hotel. Under new management and completely refurbished. The hotel dining is now in the hands of a gourmet chef. There is still entertainment in the lounges and casual barbecues on the terraces. (Reservations: 2-0331)

Castle Harbour Hotel. This large and traditional old place has dinner and dancing nightly in the *Round Table Room*. Drop in also at the *Castle Tavern* and the *Isle O'Devil's Pub,* and catch good local entertainment in the very swinging *Knight Club* off the lower rotunda. If that isn't enough the *Britannia Bar* in the *Admiralty Room* is open from 6:30 to 10 P.M. and lunch is served daily in the *Café Cascade* in the Cascade Pool area. (Reservations: 3-8161)

Grotto Bay Hotel. Down the road a bit from Castle Harbour near Tucker's Town, Grotto Bay has a pleasant dining room that is famous for its buffets. *Prospero's Cave Bar and Discotheque* on the property. (Reservations: 3-8333)

SMITH'S PARISH

Palmetto Bay Hotel. This small hotel and cottages on the edge of Harrington Sound and Flatts Village has a nice dining room and terrace for outdoor barbeques. Very friendly and Bermudian. Lively English pub in the evenings. (Reservations: 3-2323)

Pink Beach Club and Cottages. An exclusive and luxurious cottage colony with pink cottages surrounding its own private south shore beach. Definitely worth a visit to the landscaped grounds and gardens, dining room and outdoor barbecues on the terrace. (Reservations: 3-1666)

DEVONSHIRE PARISH

Ariel Sands. A pleasant cottage colony on the south shore, you can enjoy an intimate dinner and dance on the patio next to the pool. Warm and friendly. (Reservations: 2-1935)

PAGET PARISH

Elbow Beach Hotel. Something happening here every night of the week. Two seatings for dinner in the main dining room, local entertainment in the nightclub, in the *Seahorse Pub*, weekly barbecues on the terrace, and Sunday brunch from 11:30 A.M. to 2 P.M. each week. (Reservations: 5-3535)

Glencoe. Small, friendly dining room overlooking the water and local entertainment in the cozy bar. (Reservations: 1-6231)

Harmony Hall. French and Bermudian cuisine in pleasant, small restaurant. Local entertainment and dancing. (Reservations: 2-3500)

Horizons. Lovely dining room in the old Bermuda mansion on top of the hill, local entertainment and dancing. (Reservations: 5-0048)

Inverurie. Dining room overlooking the water but only a few tables can enjoy it. Sparse dinner music and bright lights. No atmosphere. Dancing on the *Marine Terrace* and entertainment in *Le Cabaret*. (Reservations: 2-1000)

Newstead. Charming dining room in old Bermuda mansion full of antiques. Very Bermudian atmosphere and hospitality in this small hotel overlooking Hamilton and the harbor. Continental food and service, plus weekly waterside barbecues and dancing on the terrace. (Reservations: 2-6060)

WARWICK PARISH

Belmont Hotel. Lots of action here in the evening. Dinner and dancing in the *Warwick Dining Room* as well as shows four times weekly (Monday, Thursday, Friday, Saturday), local entertainment in the *Harbour Lounge* twice weekly (Tuesday and Saturday), and outdoor barbecues on the terrace overlooking the Great Sound. (Reservations: 5-1301)

Flamingo Beach. Relaxed dining here in a small property overlooking the south shore and own private beach. Visitors welcome to friendly Bermudian atmosphere. (Reservations: 2-3761)

Mermaid Beach. *Miramar Restaurant* and nighttime entertainment in this small charming hotel right on the water's edge. (Reservations: 5-5031)

White Heron Country Inn. Working-class atmosphere in pub. Simple dining room. (Telephone: 8-1655)

SOUTHAMPTON PARISH

Pompano Beach Club. This small hotel has a dramatic location on a cliff above the ocean. Superb view from dining room and friendly atmosphere. (Reservations: 4-0222)

The Reefs. One of the nicest of the small hotels, tucked around its own cove on the south shore. In the summer, dine and dance on the terrace right over the ocean, weekly buffets and Sunday brunch popular. Local entertainment in the *Nautical Lounge*. (Reservations: 8-0222)

Sonesta Beach. *Port Royal Restaurant* features very good Continental cuisine. Begin the evening in the *Southampton Lounge* with its interesting mosaic mural of an old Bermuda map, and end up in the Fiddler's Green for live entertainment and fun. (Reservations: 8-8122)

Southampton Princess. What isn't there here! Stop in the *Neptune Bar*, have a gourmet dinner in the *Newport Room*, and then move on to the *Empire Room* where the most sophisticated entertainment on the island is featured. Or if you prefer a more casual evening, spend it in the *Wine Cellar* where wine, cheese and snacks are served nightly along with live entertainment. Or if you prefer the romance of surfside dining and candlelight, take the jitney down to the *Whaler Inn* for dancing on the terrace. (Reservations: 8-8000)

SANDYS PARISH

Cambridge Beaches. This is the original cottage colony on the island and has maintained its high reputation for 50 years. Dining is gracious and elegant and there are weekly barbecues, dancing and entertainment on the terrace overlooking Mangrove Bay. Dance on millstones recovered from a British ship that went down on the reefs about 1818. A perfect place for romance! (Reservations: 4-0331)

Lantana Colony Club. Very posh cottage colony overlooking the Great Sound. Lovely, Bermudian-style clubhouse with a terrace view of the water. Dining room has a "greenhouse" section that gives the illusion of dining in an arboretum. Local entertainment and dancing in the evenings. Dinner jackets suggested on Thursdays and Saturdays. (Reservations: 4-0141)

Sugar Cane Hotel. This small, informal guest house in rural Somerset, a short walk from the village and ferry landing, welcomes visitors to its dining room. Relaxed atmosphere in small, garden setting. (Reservations: 4-0989)

NIGHTCLUBS

There are several lively local nightclubs on the island that offer entertainment from about 9 P.M. until the wee hours. Some are licensed to stay open until 3 A.M. and all serve liquor to anyone over the age of 18. (This rule is strictly enforced.) Local entertainment includes limbo, calypso, steel bands as well as variety-type shows. The groups circulate around the island, so you may catch up with an act that was missed elsewhere. Both the local and hotel nightspots have a cover charge that ranges from $3 to $5 per person, but there is no minimum on how much you must spend on drinks (as a general rule). The local nightclubs are:

Clay House Inn, Devonshire. Located on the North Shore Road, this club offers steel band music, limbo and calypso in the local tradition. Shows at 10:30 P.M. and 1:00 A.M. nightly. (Reservations: 2-3193)

Flavors, Warwick Parish. Located on Riddell's Bay, just five minutes from major south shore hotels, this is one of Bermuda's most popular discotheques among the local residents. Dancing

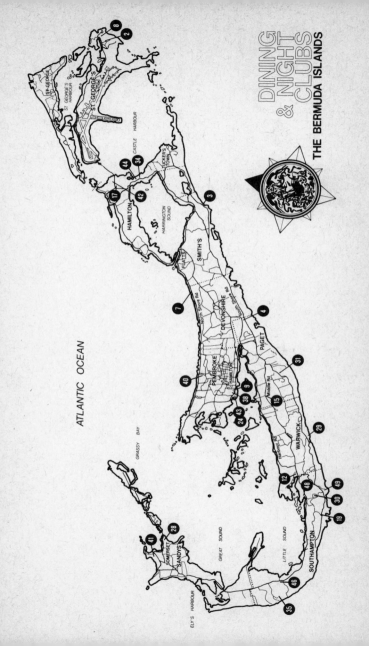

DINING
& NIGHT
CLUBS
THE BERMUDA ISLANDS

ATLANTIC OCEAN

ST. GEORGE'S
ST. GEORGE'S HARBOUR
ST. GEORGE'S HARBOUR
CASTLE HARBOUR
TUCKER'S TOWN
HAMILTON
HARRINGTON SOUND
FLATTS
SMITH'S
DEVONSHIRE
PAGET
PEMBROKE
HAMILTON
WARWICK
GRASSY BAY
GREAT SOUND
LITTLE SOUND
SOUTHAMPTON
SOMERSET
SANDYS
ELY'S HARBOUR

North Shore Rd
South Shore Rd
Middle Rd
Harbour Rd

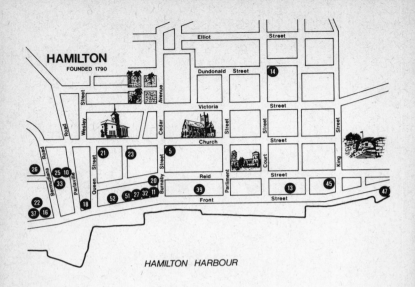

HAMILTON
FOUNDED 1790

Elliot Street

Dundonald Street

Victoria Street

Church Street

Reid Street

Front Street

Wesley Street

Road

Cedar Avenue

Burnaby Street

Parliment Street

Court Street

King Street

Bermudiana Road

Parlaville

Queen Street

26 25 10 33

21 23 5

20

18 52 51 27 32 11 39 13 45 47

22 37 16

HAMILTON HARBOUR

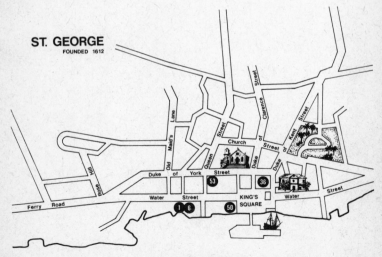

ST. GEORGE
FOUNDED 1612

Clarence Street

Old Maid's Lane

Queen Street

Church Street

Duke of Kent Street

Duke of York Street

Duke of Clarence Street

Duke of Somers Street

Rose Hill

Ferry Road

Water Street

KING'S SQUARE

53 36

1 6 50

ST. GEORGE'S HARBOUR

nightly from 9 P.M. to 3 A.M. and it is suggested that you come smartly, but casually dressed. (Reservations: 8-1987)

Disco Forty and Forty II, center of Hamilton. This nightspot on Front Street is popular with groups, especially cruise passengers, and also attracts the "in" crowd of Bermudians. Dancing from 9:30 P.M. and showtimes at 10:30 P.M. and 1:30 A.M. Open until 3 A.M. (except Sundays) and features imported acts alternating with island calypso and rock groups. (Reservations: 2-4040)

Galaxy Nightclub, town of Hamilton. Located off Front Street by the Bermudiana Hotel, this nightclub offers local and international entertainment nightly (except) Thursday until 3 A.M. (Reservations: 2-7065)

DINING AND NIGHT CLUBS

1 CROWN AND ANCHOR PUB*
2 BLACK HORSE TAVERN
3 PEDRO'S
4 IL CHIANTI
5 PAPILLON*
6 CARRIAGE HOUSE RESTAURANT*
7 CLAY HOUSE INN
8 DENNIS HIDEAWAY
9 DING-HO
10 THE CLUB
11 FISHERMAN'S REEF*
12 FLAVORS
13 DISCO FORTY & FORTY II
14 SPINNING WHEEL*
15 FOURWAYS INN
16 GALAXY NIGHTCLUB*
17 ICE CREAM PARLOUR
18 HARBOURFRONT*
19 HENRY VIII PUB-RESTAURANT
20 HOG PENNY PUB*
21 HORSE AND BUGGY*
22 LA FONTAINE*
23 LA TRATTORIA
24 LE BISTRO
25 LITTLE VENICE*
26 LOBSTER POT*
27 LONGTAIL*
28 LOYALTY INN

29 MIRAMAR
30 NEWPORT ROOM
31 PARAQUET
32 PENTHOUSE CLUB*
33 PORTOFINO
34 PLANTATION CLUB
35 PORT ROYAL GOLF CLUB
36 PUB ON THE SQUARE*
37 RAMS HEAD INN*
38 ROBIN HOOD'S RESTAURANT
39 RUM RUNNERS*
40 HAMILTONIAN HOTEL
41 SOMERSET COUNTRY SQUIRE
42 SWIZZLE INN
43 TIARA ROOM
44 TOM MOORE'S TAVERN
45 TOWN AND COUNTRY*
46 WAGON WHEEL
47 WATERFRONT*
48 WATERLOT INN
49 WHALER INN
50 WHITE HORSE TAVERN*
51 YE OLDE COCK AND FEATHER*
52 BOTANIC GARDEN
53 SAN GIORGIO RISTORANTE

*NUMBER REFERS TO DETAIL MAPS

Rum Runners, town of Hamilton. Discotheque on Front Street overlooking the harbor in *Rum Runners* restaurant. Popular among locals and open from 9 P.M. to 1 A.M. (Reservations: 2-4737)

The Club, Town of Hamilton. Recorded music in sophisticated atmosphere above *Little Venice* restaurant on Bermudiana Road. Open from 10 P.M. until 3 A.M. and restaurant patrons do not have to pay cover charge. (Reservations: 2-7091)

The Spinning Wheel, town of Hamilton. This new three-storey disco/cocktail lounge serves lunch from 12 noon to 3 P.M. during the week, on the first floor. Second floor is Disco and top is the lounge. (Reservations: 2-7799)

HOTEL NIGHTSPOTS

Belmont, Warwick Parish. Local entertainment nightly in *Warwick Room* or *Harbour Lounge* (except Sunday) at 10:15 P.M. (Reservations: 5-1301)

Bermudiana, in Hamilton. Local entertainment nightly in the *Du Barry Room* at 11:00 P.M. (except Thursday). Latest U.K. and U.S. records in the *Hoop-a-Loo Discotheque* until 3 A.M. (Reservations: 5-1211)

Castle Harbour, Tucker's Town. Local entertainment and variety shows in the *Knight Club* nightly at 10:30 P.M. Dancing until 1 A.M. (Reservations: 3-8161)

HOTEL NIGHTSPOTS

1 BELMONT HOTEL, WARWICK PARISH
2 BERMUDIANA HOTEL, TOWN OF HAMILTON
3 CASTLE HARBOUR HOTEL, TUCKER'S TOWN
4 ELBOW BEACH HOTEL, PAGET PARISH
5 GROTTO BAY HOTEL, HAMILTON PARISH
6 HOLIDAY INN, ST. GEORGE'S
7 INVERURIE HOTEL, PAGET PARISH
8 PRINCESS HOTEL, TOWN OF HAMILTON
9 SONESTA BEACH HOTEL, SOUTHAMPTON PARISH
10 SOUTHAMPTON PRINCESS HOTEL, SOUTHAMPTON PARISH

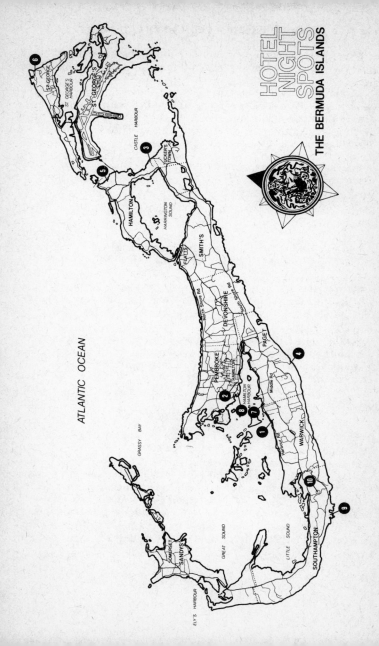

HOTEL
NIGHT
SPOTS

THE BERMUDA ISLANDS

ATLANTIC OCEAN

Elbow Beach, Paget. Local entertainment nightly except Friday. Showtime at 10 P.M. and dancing until 1 A.M. (Reservations: 5-3535)

Grotto Bay, Hamilton Parish. Local entertainment nightly in clubhouse at 10:45 P.M. *Prospero's Cave Discotheque* open from 9 P.M. to 1 A.M. (Reservations: 3-8333)

Holiday Inn, St. George's. Local entertainment nightly in *Mid-Atlantic Supper Club* and *Rainbow Lounge*. Show time at 10:30 P.M. (Reservations: 7-8222)

Inverurie, Paget Parish. Local and international entertainment nightly. Show time 10:30 P.M. (local show) and 11:30 P.M. (international show). (Reservations: 2-1000)

Princess, Hamilton. Local entertainment nightly in The *Princess Room*. Show time at 11:00 P.M. (Reservations: 5-3000)

Sonesta Beach, Southampton Parish. *Fiddler's Green* nightclub with its Electric Rainbow Light Show featuring local entertainment nightly. Show time at 10:45 P.M. (Reservations: 8-8122)

Southampton Princess, Southampton. *The Empire Room* presents top international stars and local shows nightly. Show times are 10:15 P.M. (local show) and 11:15 P.M. (international). *The Half and Half Discotheque* is open until 3 A.M. (Reservations: 8-8000)

FILMS, THEATER

There are three motion picture theaters in Bermuda—one in the center of Hamilton, one in St. George's, and one in the Village of Somerset. The *Rosebank Theater* in Hamilton now has *Cinema 1* and *2*. Several hotels also show films to their guests one night a week. Local concerts, dramatic and ballet productions are held frequently throughout the year, and the *Bermuda Festival* from mid-January to mid-February each year draws top international artists of theater, dance, opera, classical and modern music. Check the local newspapers and "This Week in Bermuda" to find the weekly calendar of events.

INDEX

INDEX

Practical Information

Place Names, Sights & Special Events